Beginning PDF
Programming with
PHP and PDFlib

By Ron Goff

php|architect
nanobooks

php|architect's Nanobook: Beginning PDFLib

Disclaimer

Bulk Copies

Marco Tabini & Associates, Inc. offers trade discounts on purchases of ten or more copies of this book. For more information, please contact our sales offices at the address or numbers below.

Credits

Written by   Ron Goff

Published by

Marco Tabini & Associates, Inc.   (416) 630-6202
28 Bombay Ave.   (877) 630-6202 toll free within North America
Toronto, ON M3H 1B7   info@phparch.com / www.phparch.com
Canada
                                    Marco Tabini, Publisher

Edited By   Martin Streicher

Technical Reviewers   Ilia Alshanetsky

Layout and Design   Arbi Arzoumani

Managing Editor   Emanuela Corso

This book is dedicated to the loving memory of my Mother.

Thanks Nadia, Zowa and Dexter – Dad (Gold Leader) - Aaron and Nellie - Frank and Julie - Everyone at Conveyor Group.

Contents

Foreword

I started the PDFlib core library back in 1997, and founded PDFlib GmbH, the company around the PDF-generating library, in 2000. Since 2001 the PDFlib distribution contains a fully supported language binding for building PDFlib as a PHP extension. This PDFlib "wrapper" (as we call it) is also included in the PHP source code distribution. When PDFlib GmbH took over maintenance of the PHP language binding for PDFlib we could build on the solid work of open-source volunteers, especially Uwe Steinmann who wrote the initial version. Consequently, PDFlib has been part of many PHP source and binary packages for many years, and provided simple PDF generation for everyone. Countless PHP developers rely on PDFlib for creating printable invoices, database reports, and other common document classes. However, the PHP/PDFlib combination proved popular in more and more application domains including preparation of PDF files for high-end printing, print-on-demand, and intra-company reporting.

While PDFlib language bindings are available for more than a dozen other environments (including COM, Java, and .NET), the PHP binding remains one of the most popular ones both for the open-source version PDFlib Lite and the full-featured commercial editions which add more advanced features on top of PDFlib Lite. Taking into account the large number of PHP developers worldwide and the highly active community which works on the PHP interpreter itself it seems that PHP will continue to play a very important role for accessing the PDFlib feature set in a Web environment. Actually, we are receiving an increasing number of reports from PDFlib users who work with PDFlib/PHP in other environments as well.

Needless to say that PDFlib GmbH is committed to maintaining the PHP wrapper for PDFlib in the future (special thanks go to Rainer Schaaf, our in-house PHP build system pundit who is responsible for the PHP wrapper, and constantly improves his build scripts in an attempt to automate the creation of gazillions of combinations of PDFlib versions, PHP versions, and operating system platforms). We are not only maintaining the existing wrapper, but also try to extend the usability of PDFlib products within the PHP world. In this spirit we introduced an object-oriented language binding when PHP 5 pushed the object-oriented paradigm. Currently we are working on an extended wrapper version which will leverage the upcoming Unicode support in future versions of PHP. Also, other PDFlib GmbH products in addition to the core PDFlib, such as our PDFlib PLOP (PDF Linearization, Optimization, Privacy) and the Text Extraction Toolkit (PDFlib TET) provide PHP wrappers as well.

Numerous books have been published to serve the needs of the PHP community, and most of these include a few pages on PDFlib. However, I am happy to see Ron Goff's book which is the first that is fully devoted to using PDFlib from within PHP. I hope it will reach many readers and make their everyday programming work a bit easier.

Thomas Merz
President
PDFlib GmbH

About the Author

Ron is the technical director/senior programmer for Conveyor Group (www.conveyorgroup.com), a Southern-California based web development firm. He is the author of several articles for PHP|Architect magazine and other online publications. Ron's lives in California with his wife Nadia and 2 children. You can contact him at ron@conveyorgroup.com.

Introduction

THE PORTABLE DOCUMENT FORMAT, or PDF, has become the international de facto standard for electronic document distribution. The PDF format retains the formatting and flow of a document much better than any other format, and because PDF can embed fonts, illustrations, and images, readers see exactly what the author (or publisher) intended.

More and more computer applications, especially Web applications, need the ability to produce high quality PDF files for invoices, reports, newsletters, and even proofs of traditional printed magazines. In some cases, PDFs have to be created on-the-fly. For example, many publishers now sell books online as PDF files and "stamp" each copy sold with the name and email address of the purchaser. (Some publishers also secure each copy with its own unique password.)

There are a number of commercial and open source software packages suitable for on-demand PDF generation, including *Free PDF, PC4P,* and *PHP*

PDF Creation. One of the best packages is *PDF Library*, the software this book focuses on.

The PDF Library, or *PDFlib*, has been available since 1997. It is a feature-rich application program interface (API) that's fast, robust, and capable of creating hundreds of professional, accurate, and high-resolution PDFs on well-trafficked Web servers and in mission-critical applications. *PDFlib* is available for many programming and scripting languages, including PHP, and completely shields the programmer from the intricacies of creating a PDF from scratch.

The PDFlib Company

PDFlib is offered and maintained by PDFlib, GmbH (`http://pdflib.com`), a company founded at the start of the new millennium to make *PDFlib* a professional product. The company offers many products for generating PDFs, and which one you choose depends on your specific needs. All of the packages create PDFs, but some have advanced capabilities. For example, a limited version if PDFlib, *PDFlib Lite* written in *C*, is available as open source. At the other extreme, the *PDFlib Personalization Server* (PPS), can create high-quality, variable-data PDFs.

Here's a brief breakdown of the different products available from PDFlib. Complete information and product comparisons can be found at the PDFlib web site.

PDFlib Lite

PDFlib Lite, the open source product, is free to download and use if you're an open source or research developer, and provides the ability to create very basic PDFs. It doesn't include more advanced capabilities for formatting, such as embedding font subsets, handling and reflowing text, and so on. However, you need to create very simple PDFs, PDFlib Lite should suffice.

Precompiled PDFlib with PHP

Some versions of PHP come with PDFlib precompiled and ready to run. This version of PDFlib is based on PDFlib Lite and also has limited features as compared to the full version of PDFlib (described next).

PDFlib

PDFlib is the standard library. This package contains all of the basics necessary to create a PDF, and also includes advanced features, including text formatting, optimization, security, and much more. PDFlib is perfect for creating complex, high-quality PDFs from the ground up.

PDFlib + PDI

PDFlib + PDI contains the standard PDFlib library, but also includes the ability to (re)process already-made PDFs. This is extremely useful for placing or even resizing premade PDF files within another PDF document or even merging several PDFs together. If you need to work with pre-built PDFs, this is the product to choose.

PDFlib Personalization Server

Based on PDFlib + PDI, the *PDFlib Personalization Server* (PPS) adds one big feature: the ability to incorporate variable data within designated areas of existing PDFs. The *PDFlib Block* tool is combined with *Adobe Acrobat Professional* to control how variable data should display in specific areas. Given such a PDF "template", PPS can inject data dynamically to create custom PDFs on demand.

Plop

Linearization (which delivers the first pages of a large PDF while the rest of the document is downloaded), optimization, and security are three great features that are not found in PDFlib Lite. However, *Plop* gives you the ability to apply these three features on existing PDFs whether the PDFs were created with PDFlib or not. Plop also provides a command-line utility to batch-process existing PDFs.

All in all, the products offered by PDFlib are very robust and are built to give you great control over the creation and manipulation of PDFs without sacrificing performance. PDFlib was designed to create thousands of high-quality PDFs very, very quickly. Even if you create just a few PDFs per month, you'll still appreciate its speed and robustness.

1

Installation

INSTALLING *PDFlib version 6*, the latest version of PDFlib, is relatively easy. Just download one of the precompiled PDFlib modules (PDFlib Lite is the only product not offered as a precompiled module, as it's available solely as source code), drop it in your PHP extensions directory, and then either call it on every use or edit your *php.ini* to load the extension automatically.

PDFlib version 6 works only with *PHP version 4.3.0* (and above) and *PHP version 5.0*. Future releases of PDFlib may work with *PHP version 5.1* and newer releases; check the PDFlib web site periodically for updates.

Building PDFlib from source
You can obtain the source code for any version of PDFlib and compile your own library from scratch. However, because the steps to build PDFlib and PHP from source can be complicated and specific to your hardware and operating system, this book won't describe the process.

Obtaining PDFlib

You can download the PDFlib software from http://www.pdflib.com. The site offers a unique package for each major operating system (and some specialized hardware), and also offers small, add-on packages that bind the main package to specific programming languages.

If you download and use one of the pre-built PDFlib libraries, you can develop, test, and demonstrate your application without purchasing a license — an incredibly useful feature to evaluate the library and refine specifications with a client — but each PDF you generate will display a non-editable "stamp" that render the documents unusable in a production environment. Purchasing a license removes the stamp.

Once you've downloaded the appropriate *.zip*, *.tar*, or *.dmg* file (for Windows, Linux, and Mac OS X, respectively), unpack the compressed file to extract PDFlib, the documentation (in English), and sample programs (for all languages). (Optionally, Windows developers can download all of the necessary software from http://snaps.php.net)

The module for PHP 4.3.x can be found in the directory *bind/php4/php-430;* the module for *PHP 4.4.x* is in the directory *bind/php4/php-440;* and the module for *PHP 5.0* can be found in *bind/php5/php-503* . Once you've found the correct module for your version of PHP, you're ready to proceed.

Installing the PDFlib for PHP

PDFlib can be included in a PHP application via PHP's dl() function or via *php.ini.* The latter technique provides ubiquitous access and may be preferable since the former method doesn't work in safe mode or if the *php.ini* parameter enable_dl is disabled. Moreover, dl() has been deprecated as of PHP 4, and enable_dl is typically disabled on shared hosts. Changing *php.ini* is also better for running PDFlib on PHP 5.

No matter which method you choose, you must first copy the PDFlib module to your extensions folder. Copy the PDFlib module, *libpdf_php.so* (on Linux) or *libpdf_php.dll* (on Windows), into the PHP extensions folder on your server. To find your extensions directory, look at the extension_dir parameter in your *php.ini.* (On Linux, the default location is */usr/local/php/lib/php/extensions/;* on Windows, the default directory is *C:\php4\extensions*.)

The dl() Method

Using the dl () method is definitely the simplest way to run PDFlib (but beware of the caveats listed immediately above). Every time you need to use PDFlib in your PHP code, call the dl () function. You should also check that the extension isn't already loaded by using the extension_loaded() function. (Re-loading an extension causes an error.)

```
// On Linux platforms, write…
if (!extension_loaded('pdf')) {
  dl("libpdf_php.so")
}

// On Windows, write…
if (!extension_loaded('pdf')) {
  dl("libpdf_php.dll")
}
```

The php.ini Method

To include PDFlib every time PDF is started, insert one of the following lines, depending on your operating system, into the *php.ini* file.

```
// On Linux, add the line…
extension=libpdf_php.so

// On Windows, add the line…
extension=libpdf_php.dll
```

After adding the line, restart your Web server (Apache or IIS, say) to make the change take effect. (You do not have to restart the Web server if you're using the PHP CGI or the CLI SAPIs.) You can now use all of the powerful features of PDFlib (although a stamp will appear until you've purchased an official license).

(i) | **Rebuilding with PEAR & PECL**
You can also rebuild your version of PDFlib using *PECl*. The site http://pecl. php.net contains the file needed to build the PDFlib extension. Download the file and run the following on your server:

```
pear install pecl/pdflib-2.0.tgz
```

Locate where you've installed the latest version of PDFlib, which may be *pdflib/bind/c*, and the rest is automatic.

Obtaining and Using a License Key

To purchase a license key, go to http://pdflib.com. You can either mail your order using the supplied purchase order form or purchase a license key online. After obtaining your key, reference it every time you use PDFlib in your code:

```
PDF_set_parameter($p, "license", "REPLACE THIS TEXT WITH YOUR LI-
CENSE KEY");
```

After you set the license key within your application, you can only access the PDFlib features that you've paid for. However, you can re-enable all of the available features at any time by using 0 ("zero") as a license key. The zero also re-enables the stamp.

```
PDF_set_parameter($p, "license", "0");
```

Summary

Installing PDFlib isn't difficult. Choosing the precompiled versions of the PDFlib modules is far easier than recompiling and reinstalling PHP with PDFlib. Furthermore, using the precompiled modules makes upgrades to newer versions of PDFlib just as easy as the first install.

2

Creating Your First PDF

WHILE CREATING A PDF FROM your favorite desktop word processor is usually quite easy, creating a PDF from a Web application is a little more complicated. Even though *PDFlib* hides most of the gory details of generating a PDF behind its convenient programming interface, there are still a number of formatting options and variables to consider and control.

At first, PDFlib may seem like a large dragon, awe-inspiring in size and terribly powerful. Indeed, there are many facets to PDFlib—many options and choices—but set aside your trepidation. Any PHP developer can tame PDFlib.

Hello World

Let's begin by creating a PDF with the standard "Hello World" message. (You can find the complete code in *listing_ch_2.php* and *listing_ch_2_P54.php*. The former file is based on the latest versions of PDFlib and PHP. Refer to the latter file if you're using a *PDFlib version 5* or a version of PHP 4 with PDFlib compiled in.)

```php
<?php
if (!extension_loaded('pdf')) {
  dl('libpdf_php.so');
}

$p = PDF_new();

PDF_begin_document($p, "", "");

PDF_set_info($p, "Creator", "my_first_pdf.php");
PDF_set_info($p, "Author", "Ron Goff");
PDF_set_info($p, "Title", "My First PDF from PDFlib");

PDF_begin_page_ext($p, 612, 792, "");

$font = PDF_load_font($p, "Helvetica", "winansi", "");
PDF_setfont($p, $font, 30);
PDF_set_text_pos($p, 10, 700);
PDF_show($p, "Hello World.");

PDF_end_page_ext($p, "");
PDF_end_document($p, "");

$buf = PDF_get_buffer($p);
$len = strlen($buf);

header("Content-type: application/pdf");
if ($_SERVER["SERVER_PORT"] == "443" &&
    (strpos($_SERVER["HTTP_USER_AGENT"], 'MSIE') !== false)) {
  header("Cache-Control: must-revalidate, post-check=0, pre-
check=0", 1);
  header("Pragma: public", 1);
}

header("Content-Length: $len");
header("Content-Disposition: inline; filename=hello_world.pdf");
print $buf;

PDF_delete($p);
?>
```

The first step is to invoke the dl() method, but only if you haven't installed PDFlib using the *php.ini* method and aren't using a version of PHP with PDFlib compiled in. (The use of dl() is not recommended; see Chapter 1, "Installing

PDFlib", to learn how to install PDFlib using *php.ini* instead.)

```
if (!extension_loaded('pdf')) {
  dl("libpdf_php.so")
}
```

To avoid an error, !extension_loaded('pdf') ensures that the PDFlib extension has not already been loaded.

With the extension loaded, the next step is to create a new, blank PDF:

```
$p = PDF_new();
PDF_begin_document($p, "", "");
```

Code Variation

If you're using PDFlib 5 or PHP 4 precompiled with PDFlib, call the PDF_open_file() function instead of PDF_begin_document().

$p = PDF_new();
// PDFlib 5 or PHP 4 precompiled with PDFlib
PDF_open_file($p, "");

PDF_begin_document() is a very versatile function, used to set passwords, optimizations, and many other settings. (The next chapter presents more advanced examples.) Here, the only parameter needed is the handle to the document, $p. No filename is given either, so the PDF can be immediately displayed in the browser.

Next, each of the subsequent three lines, the three calls to pdf_set_info(), set annotations that appear in the off-screen description portion of the PDF. Such annotations aren't required, but are useful to record copyright information, the creator of the PDF (you or your application), and other information that need not appear in the readable document itself.

```
PDF_set_info($p, "Creator", "my_first_pdf.php");
PDF_set_info($p, "Author", "Ron Goff");
PDF_set_info($p, "Title", "My First PDF from PDFlib");
```

The next step is to specify the physical dimensions of the document. This example specifies the dimensions in *Postscript points*. One Postscript point is approximately 0.0138 inches. Hence, a standard 8.5" by 11" piece of paper measures 612x792 Postscript points. PDF_begin_page_ext() sets the page size.

```
PDF_begin_page_ext($p, 612, 792, "");
```

Code Variation

For those using PDFlib 5 or PDFlib precompiled with PHP 4, use the PDF_begin_page() function instead of the PDF_being_page_ext() function.

// PDFlib 5 or PHP 4 precompiled with PDFlib
PDF_begin_page($p, 612, 792);

The next two lines set the font for the sample text. This sample uses the default *Helvetica* font that comes with PDF, and sets the font size at 30. (PDF includes a very few standard fonts, but you can embed other fonts to keep the look and flow of your documents intact.)

```
$font = PDF_load_font($p, "Helvetica", "winansi", "");
PDF_setfont($p, $font, 30);
```

Code Variation

If you're coding with the PDFlib precompiled with PHP 4, you may have to use the PDF_findfont() function instead of the PDF_load_font() function. PDF_findfont() works in PDFlib 5, but it's preferable to use PDF_load_font().

...Continued

```
// PHP 4 precompiled with PDFlib
$font = PDF_findfont($p, "Helvetica", "winansi", "");
PDF_setfont($p, $font, 30);
```

The line PDF_set_text_pos() positions the pointer where text should begin. The position of the pointer is expressed in Postscript points and the origin of the pointer is the *bottom left corner* of each page. For example, to render text very close to the bottom left corner, you'd write:

```
PDF_set_text_pos($p, 1, 1);
```

However, for this example, the pointer is placed at the top-left of the page with Postscript point coordinates (10,700):

```
PDF_set_text_pos($p, 10, 700);
```

Now, draw the text "Hello, World" with PDF_show():

```
PDF_show($p, "Hello World.");
```

Just two more steps to go—close the page and close the document:

```
PDF_end_page_ext($p, "");
PDF_end_document($p, "");
```

Code Variation

If your application uses PDFlib 5 or PHP 4 PDFlib precompiled with PDFlib, use the PDF_end_page() and PDF_close() functions instead of PDF_page_ext() and PDF_end_document().

```
PDF_end_page($p);
PDF_close($p);
```

The next step is to place all of PDF data into a buffer that can be sent to the browser. $buf is the buffer and $len is set to the length of the buffer.

```
$buf = PDF_get_buffer($p);
$len = strlen($buf);
```

The next lines add the headers required to invoke the browser's PDF plug-in. (One of the headers, Cache-Control, fixes a bug in *Internet Explorer*. Without Cache-Control, the page is displayed incorrectly). PDF_delete() removes the PDF from memory.

```
header("Content-type: application/pdf");
if ($_SERVER["SERVER_PORT"] == "443" &&
    (strpos($_SERVER["HTTP_USER_AGENT"], 'MSIE') !== false)) {
  header("Cache-Control: must-revalidate, post-check=0, pre-
check=0", 1);
  header("Pragma: public", 1);
}
header("Content-Length: $len");
header("Content-Disposition: inline; filename=hello_world.pdf");
print $buf;

PDF_delete($p);
```

If you try this example, the browser automatically launches its PDF plug-in to display the page. The browser won't change the URL of the page, but if you decide to save the PDF, the file's default name will be *hello_world.pdf*, because that's the file name specified in its PDF header.

Saving to Disk

Displaying a generated PDF in the browser saves your users effort and disk space, because the end-user isn't required to save the PDF and then open it in another application. However, if you want users to save the PDF, the example code needs only a few tweaks to make that work. In fact, it takes *less* code to save the PDF.

First, set the file name in PDF_begin_document():

```
PDF_begin_document($p, " hello_world.pdf", "");
```

Code Variation

Use PDF_open_file() to name the file instead of PDF_begin_document() if you're using PDFlib 5 or PHP 4 precompiled with PDFlib.

```
PDF_open_file($p, "hello.pdf");
```

Then, after PDF_end_document(), immediately call PDF_delete(), which causes the file to be saved to disk.

```
PDF_end_document($p, "");
PDF_delete($p);
```

Code Variation

Again, the instructions for saving the file vary slightly if you're programming with PDFlib 5 or PHP 4 precompiled with PDFlib: call the PDF_end_page() and PDF_close() functions instead of the PDF_page_ext() and PDF_end_document() function.

```
PDF_close($p);
PDF_delete($p);
```

3

Formatting with PDFlib

P DF documents generated from *PDFlib* can be simple or complicated. In this chapter, let's explore some of the formatting capabilities PDFlib has to offer and learn how to use a new PDFlib feature that flows text automatically.

Color Management

PDFlib supports many different color systems, so you can precisely match colors to a pre-existing design or to a company's style sheet. PDFlib supports grayscale, "red, green, and blue" (RGB), "cyan, magenta, yellow, black" (CMYK), CIE L*A*B*, *PANTONE*, and *HKS* spot color.

To specify a color, you must set three parameters: the "pen", the color system (for example, RGB or HKS), and the color value.

The pen can be set to fill, stroke, or both. As its name implies, fill fills the text or shape with color. stroke draws only the outline in the specified color, and both renders the inside and outline of the shape or text in the color.

The color system is one of the color systems listed immediately above, such as rgb or cmyk.

The color value specifies an exact color in the context of the chosen color system. If you do not set the color system correctly, the color you choose may not be displayed correctly.

CMYK

To specify a CMYK color, provide the cyan, magenta, yellow, and black components of the color. Each component must be expressed as a decimal value between 0 and 1. To compute the proper decimal value, divide each component by 255.

For example, if you want to use dark red, which has a CMYK value of (0, 153, 153, 102), divide each value by 255 to yield 0, 0.6, 0,6, and 0.4, respectively. Next, call PDF_setcolor():

```
PDF_setcolor($p, "both", "cmyk", 0, 0.6, 0.6, 0.4);
```

RGB

Similar to CMYK, RGB colors are also specified as a series of saturations. RGB colors are expressed by three saturations: the red, green, and blue component of the chosen color. You can express the saturations in hexidecimal or decimal.

If you want to specify the RGB value in decimal (a value such as (225, 0, 13), then provide each component as a percentage of 255:

```
PDF_setcolor($p, "both", "rgb", 225/255, 0/255, 13/255, 0);
```

PANTONE

Setting a PANTONE spot color is a little bit different. You must first create a spot color with PDF_makespotcolor() and then call PDF_setcolor() to use that color.

To create the spot color, you must know the PANTONE color number and the type of paper you want to use—for example, PANTONE color 245 (a light purple) on coated paper. Using the PANTONE guide, find that combination: the proper color to specify is "PANTONE 245 C". Given that name, call PDF_makespotcolor():

```
$spot = PDF_makespotcolor($p, "PANTONE 245 C");
```

PDF_makespotcolor() returns a spot color reference to use in PDF_setcolor().

To call PDF_setcolor(), provide the spot color reference and the amount of color tint as a percentage. For example, to use "PANTONE 245 C" at 100% tint, use the call:

```
PDF_setcolor($p, "both", "spot", $spot, 1, 0, 0);
```

Here, the color system is spot, the next argument, $spot, is the spot color previously returned from PDF_makespotcolor(), and the 1 (numeral "one") represents a tint of 100%. (A tint of 60% would be represented as 0.6.)

The two trailing zeroes in the function call are *placeholders*. If a color system doesn't use four color components (as CMYK does), any "unused" arguments to the function must be 0. (If you're upgrading your application to PDFlib version 6, you may have to update your code to the new function interface—especially if you previously used RGB colors.)

ⓘ **PDFlib Lite Exception**
The PDF_makespotcolor() is not available in the PDFlib lite version.

Putting It All Together

Given the basics so far, let's render a text string in a dark green CMYK color.

```
PDF_setcolor($p, "both", "cmyk", 0.4, 0, 0.26, 0.6);
PDF_set_text_pos($p, 20, 650);
PDF_show($p, "The fish was delish and it made quite a dish.");
```

The pen is both, the color system is cmyk, and the remaining arguments are the four components of the CMYK color expressed as values between 0 and 1.

You can display as many different colors as you'd like in a PDF. In fact, each element—a piece of text or a shape—can be a different color, if need be.

Displaying Text

There are several ways within PDFlib to display text. As of version 6, there's also a new tool to flow text correctly—a really important feature when working with large blocks of text.

An Alternative Way to Display Text

You've already seen one example of displaying text in the previous chapter. PDF_set_text_pos() set the pointer, and PDF_show() created the text.

```
PDF_set_text_pos($p, 10, 700);
PDF_show($p, "Hello World.");
```

PDF_show_xy() is a shortcut that combines PDF_set_text_pos() and PDF_show(). The following line of code is equivalent to the two lines of code above:

```
PDF_show_xy($p, "Hellow, World", 10, 700);
```

If you want a little more flexibility, use PDF_fit_textline(). It has many options to control the behavior of a line of text.

For example, if you'd like to rotate the text slightly and change the color of the font, you can do that in one call to PDF_fit_textline():

```
PDF_fit_textline($p, "Hey hey hey", 100,  200,  "rotate=10
fillcolor={rgb
0.2 0.4 1}");
```

Code Variation

The PDF_fit_textline() function *is not* available in the PDFlib version pre-compiled with PHP 4. However, PDFlib 5 provides the function, but with one exception: PDF_fit_textline() doesn't accept the fillcolor option. Instead, the color must be set before the function is called.

```
// PDFlib version 5
PDF_setcolor($p, "both", "rgb", 0.2, 0.4, 1);
PDF_fit_textline($p, "Hey hey hey", 100,  200,  "rotate=10");
```

Continuing Text

When you need to continue a sentence or paragraph below the previous line, use PDF_continue_text(). The position and font style of the text are automatically set based on the most recent call to PDF_show(), PDF_show_xy(), PDF_fit_textline(), or PDF_set_text_pos(). Hence, this code prints a line to the PDF and then continues the text on a subsequent line:

```
PDF_set_text_pos($p, 20, 650);
PDF_show($p, "The fish was delish and it made quite a dish.");
PDF_continue_text($p, "But the pork I ate with a fork, not a
spork.");
```

Flowing Text

One of the latest additions to PDFlib is the ability to *flow* text correctly. Just like desktop publishing software, PDFlib can automatically fit and wrap styled text to the constraints of a specified area. Using this feature requires some additional steps but it's incredibly flexible. For instance, you can change the attributes of text within a flow, assigning a different color to every letter, say.

Let's create a small box with the sentence "The fish was delish and made quite a dish" flowed over a few lines. To begin, create a flow with PDF_create_textflow(), specifying the text, the font, the paragraph's alignment, and other settings:

```
$sample_text = "The fish was delish and made quite a dish";
$textbox = PDF_create_textflow($p, $sample_text, "alignment=left
leading=100%
   fontname=Helvetica fontsize=12 fillcolor={rgb 1 .54 0}
encoding=winansi");
```

Next, set the size and other attributes of the flow's rectangular region and render the text with PDF_fit_textflow():

```
PDF_fit_textflow($p, $textbox, 75, 600, 150, 500, "showborder");
```

Here, the showborder option reveals the border of the text box. Finally, use PDF_delete_textflow() to remove the flow object that was just created:

```
PDF_delete_textflow($p, $textbox);
```

Being able to reflow text in a document is important when working with long strings and especially if an end-user is dynamically producing the text, say, in a form.

Inline Option

To change text attributes anywhere within a string of text, use *inline options*, also new to PDF_fit_textflow(). *Inline options* let you embolden words and change font and font color mid-sentence, among other effects. Tags resemble

HTML tags and can specify as many text attributes as you need.

For instance, to change a word in a sentence to red and bold type, embed a *inline option* as follows:

```
$sample_text = "The fish was <fillcolor={rgb 1 0 0}
 fontname=Helvetica-BoldOblique encoding= winansi >delish <
 fillcolor={rgb 0 0 0} fontname=Helvetica-BoldOblique encoding=
 winansi >and made quite a dish";
```

The first inline option, <fillcolor={rgb 1 0 0}... >, changes the color and type-face of the text delish. Once you change font properties in an *inline option*, the effects persist until you specify a new set of font properties. The second inline option, <{fillcolor={rgb 0 0 0}...>, resets the color and typeface back to black and normal, respectively. You can also use the "<resetfont>" tag to revert to the default font settings. However, it's best to reset the font attributes manually, as seen in the example.

Creating Shapes

PDFlib allows you to create any shape. You also have the option to fill the shape with color or just stroke the outline.

Let's look at how to create two basic shapes: a circle using the PDF_cir-cle() function and a rectangle using the function PDF_lineto().

Creating a Circle

When creating a shape, you first set its color using the PDF_setcolor() and set the width of the shape's outline with PDF_setlinewidth(). (Line width is obviously more important if you aren't filling the shape with the same color as its outline.) Next, you create the circle using PDF_circle(), and draw the shape with PDF_fill() or PDF_stroke() to fill the shape with color or just draw the shape's outline, respectively.

This code draws a filled, colored circle:

```
PDF_setcolor($p, "both", "cmyk", 0, 0.54, 0.70, 0.24);
```

```
PDF_setlinewidth($p, 2);
PDF_circle($p, 200, 500, 30);
PDF_fill($p);
```

The call PDF_circle($p, 200, 500, 30) displays a circle centered at position (200,500) with a radius of 30 points. If you want to display just the outline of the circle, change the last line to PDF_stroke($p).

Creating a Rectangle

To create a quadrilateral, you move the pointer to a starting position using PDF_moveto() and then draw three sides of the quadrilateral with calls to PDF_lineto(), moving from one position to another. For example, this code draws a filled rectangle:

```
PDF_setlinewidth($p, 2);
PDF_moveto($p,150,500);
PDF_lineto($p,500,500);
PDF_lineto($p,500,300);
PDF_lineto($p,150,300);
PDF_fill($p);
```

You can create any shape using a series of calls to PDF_lineto().

Placing an Image

Placing an image is a fairly easy process and PDFlib supports many popular image formats, including *GIF, BMP, CCITT, PNG, JPEG, TIFF,* and raw image formats. PDF_fit_image() gives you many options to control the placement of images, such as position, size, and rotation.

To place an image, first load it using PDF_load_image(). If you use auto as the second argument, the function automatically detects the image type, unless the image is a CCITT or raw image. If you're working with the latter two formats or if you want to specify an exact type, then use one of the keywords ccitt, raw, gif, bmp, png, jpeg, or tiff.

With the image loaded, you place the image at an *(x,y)* coordinate, and optionally rotate and scale the image. In the code below, the file *image.jpg* is loaded, placed at (100, 50), rotated 90 degrees and scaled to half (0.5) its original size. (Rotating an image *D* degrees, where *D* is a positive integer, rotates the image *D* degrees *counterclockwise*; to rotate the image clockwise, use a negative integer.)

```
$imagefile = "image.jpg";
$image = PDF_load_image($p, "auto", $imagefile, "");
PDF_fit_image($p, $image, 100, 50, "rotate=90 scale=0.5");
PDF_close_image($p, $image);
```

The final step is to close the image with PDF_close_image(). Closing an image frees the memory associated with the picture.

rotate rotates the image around its bottom-left corner placed at *(x, y)*. Depending on the values of *x* and *y* and the degree of rotation, an image can be clipped if a portion of the image ultimately falls outside of the page. For example, *Figure 1* shows an image rotated 180 degrees using rotate.

Another option to rotate your image is to use the orientate option. Orientate first rotates the image and then places the new bottom-left corner at *(x,y)*. *Figure 2* shows how orientate=south, the equivalent of a 180-degree rotation, would look placed at the same *(x,y)* as the image in *Figure 1*.

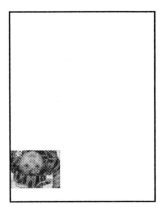

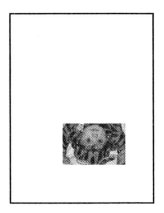

Figure 1 Rotating an image around (x,y) using rotate

Figure 2 Rotating an image around (x,y) using orientate

Until you call PDF_close_image(), you can use the same image over and over again on multiple pages. Each use of the image is independent. So, for example, if you rotate the image 90 degrees on one page, you don't have to rotate it back before placing it anew.

Keep in mind that each "open" image takes up memory. If you're using many large images, it may be prudent to close each image before using the next.

Placing Bookmarks

Adding a basic bookmark to an individual PDF page is done simply by calling the PDF_create_bookmark() function immediately after the section that you want to bookmark. There is no limit to the amount of bookmarks and sub-bookmarks a PDF can contain.

For instance, if you want to place a bookmark on a page that contains a circle, first draw the circle and then create the bookmark:

```
PDF_setlinewidth($p, 2.0);
PDF_circle($p, 200, 500, 30);
PDF_fill($p);
PDF_create_bookmark($p, "Circle", "");
```

This creates a bookmark named Circle that's linked to the page that contains the circle.

In some circumstances, you may need to create sub-bookmarks, or children of a main bookmark. For example, perhaps a page contains a number of circles and you'd like to create a main bookmark Circles and sub-bookmarks Red Circle, Blue Circle, and so on, for each individual circle. You can create a sub-bookmark by adding the option parent=1. This creates a sub-bookmark under the main level of bookmarks.

```
PDF_setlinewidth($p, 2.0);
PDF_circle($p, 200, 500, 30);
PDF_fill($p);
PDF_create_bookmark($p, "Circle", "");
```

```
PDF_setcolor($p, "both", "rgb", 1, 0, 0, 0);
PDF_setlinewidth($p, 2.0);
PDF_circle($p, 200, 500, 30);
PDF_fill($p);
PDF_create_bookmark($p, "Red Circle", "parent=1");
```

The number after parent= represents the handle of the main bookmark. For example, you can create sub-bookmarks of sub-bookmarks using the parent option:

```
PDF_create_bookmark($p, "Red Circle 1", "parent=1");
PDF_create_bookmark($p, "Red Circle 2", "parent=2");
```

The code above creates the sub-bookmark Red Circle 2 under Red Circle 1, which is under the main bookmark Circle. The hierarchy of bookmarks which would look like this within the PDF:

```
Circle
          Red Circle 1
                Red Circle 2
```

When creating a sub-bookmark you also have the option to have that sub-bookmark expanded by default or collapsed under a main bookmark. Adding open=true as an option expands the bookmark.

```
PDF_create_bookmark($p, "Red Circle", "parent=1 open=true");
```

All sub-bookmarks are collapsed by default.

Code Variation

To place a bookmark in PDFlib 5 or PDFlib precompiled with PHP4, use the function `PDF_add_bookmark()`. This function works similarly to `PDF_create_bookmark()`, except that the second to the last field only accepts a number to represent the parent. The last field only accepts a digit to specify the submenu being opened or collapsed.

```
// PDFlib5 or PDFlib precompiled with PHP 4 example
PDF_add_bookmark($p, "Red Circle 1", 0, 1);
PDF_add_bookmark($p, "Red Circle 2", 1, 0);
```

Multiple Pages

Most PDF documents contain multiple pages and sometimes need multiple page sizes. To create multiple pages, open a page, add its contents, close the page, and repeat that process for each page you want to create. You can add as many pages as you need, and each page can be a different size.

For instance, this code creates a standard 8.5" x 11" initial page and then creates a smaller second page:

```
PDF_begin_page_ext($p, 612, 792, "");
$font = PDF_load_font($p, "Helvetica", "winansi", "");
PDF_setfont($p, $font, 30);
PDF_show_xy($p, "Hey hey hey", 100, 200);
PDF_end_page_ext($p, "");

PDF_begin_page_ext($p, 550, 600, "");
$font = PDF_load_font($p, "Helvetica", "winansi", "");
PDF_setfont($p, $font, 30);
PDF_show_xy($p, "Hey hey hey on page 2", 100, 200);
PDF_end_page_ext($p, "");
```

Code Variation

Here is the same example for those using PDFlib 5 or PDFlib precompiled with PHP4.

```
// PDFlib5 or PDFlib precompiled with PHP 4 example
PDF_begin_page($p, 612, 792);
$font = PDF_findfont($p, "Helvetica", "winansi", 0);
```
...Continued

```
PDF_setfont($p, $font, 30);
PDF_show_xy($p, "Hey hey hey", 100, 200);
PDF_end_page($p);
PDF_begin_page($p, 550, 600);
$font = PDF_findfont($p, "Helvetica", "winansi", 0);
PDF_setfont($p, $font, 30);
PDF_show_xy($p, "Hey hey hey on page 2", 100, 200);
PDF_end_page($p);
```

Chapter Summary

Given all of the formatting options that PDFlib offers, you can create just about any kind of document. This chapter provides an overview of some of the options, but there are lots of variables and options in each PDFlib function for you to discover. See the PDFlib documentation for all of the details and features.

4
Font
Management

FONT MANAGEMENT IS CRUCIAL to the creation of a PDF. If fonts aren't handled properly, the PDF that you create won't reproduce accurately. *PDFlib* offers many functions to manage fonts.

Standard Core Fonts

PDF document viewers such as Adobe's *Acrobat Reader* include fourteen core fonts: Helvetica, Helvetica-Bold, Helvetica-Oblique, and Helvetica-Bold-Oblique; Courier, Courier-Bold, Courier-Oblique, and Courier-BoldOblique; Times-Roman, Times-Bold, Times-Italic, and Times-BoldItalic; and Symbol and ZapfDingbats.

These fourteen fonts don't need to be embedded in a PDF, and you don't need to install these core fonts on the server that's generating PDFs with PDFlib. You also don't need a license to use these fonts.

To load one of the core fonts, call PDF_load_font():

```
$font = PDF_load_font($p, "Helvetica", "winansi", "");
```

In the function call, The second argument is the full name of the font, the third argument is the *encoding* (discussed below), and the fourth argument allows you to set discretionary options.

> **Code Variation**
> To load fonts in PDFlib precompiled in PHP4 you will have to use the PDF_ findfont() function.
>
> ```
> // PDFlib precompiled with PHP 4 example
> $font = PDF_findfont($p, "Helvetica", "winansi", 0);
> ```

Encoding

Encoding a font interprets the font's characters for a specific language or platform. If you choose the wrong encoding for a certain font, your text will be displayed as garbage. Additionally, some fonts may only have an encoding for the Macintosh. If a Mac-specific font is embedded in a PDF, it will probably not display correctly on a Windows machine.

The encoding winansi interprets a font for Microsoft Windows. macroman, which stands for "Macintosh Roman," is used to interpret a font on *Mac OS System 9*. Mac OS X deprecates macroman and instead uses Unicode, the standardized, universal encoding that provides multi-language support for any system.

Instead of specifying a particular encoding, you can choose to use the special encodings host or auto. Using either forces PDFlib to try to deduce a proper encoding based on what operating system PDFlib is running on.

```
$font = PDF_load_font($p, "Helvetica", "host", "");
```

If you're producing PDF files on the same platform your readers tend to use, the auto or host option may be very practical. However, if your server is a Linux machine and you choose auto and your readers use Windows, the PDF may not work. Alternatively, if you're running on Windows and choose winansi, the PDF should be viewable on all platforms.

In general, the results of auto and host are somewhat unreliable, and ultimately host and auto should be avoided if possible.

Code Variation

To load fonts in PDFlib precompiled in PHP4, you will have to use the PDF_findfont() function.

```
// PDFlib precompiled with PHP 4 example
$font = PDF_findfont($p, "Helvetica", "host", 0);
```

Embedding Fonts

The fourteen core fonts found in all PDF software are useful, but it's quite likely that your documents will use other, much more novel and attractive fonts. However, because not every end-user is guaranteed to have the exact same set of fonts as your system, typefaces other than the core fonts must be *embedded* documents, that use the fonts. Embedding a font copies every character in the font into the internals of the PDF document itself. When the PDF is subsequently viewed, the stored characters are retrieved and rendered by the reader software to accurately reproduce the look of document.

Check Your Font License

Before you embed a font, check the font's license. You may not be permitted to embed the font. Some fonts do not allow embedding because an end-user can edit the PDF, essentially using the font without a proper license.

To embed a *TrueType* or *OpenType* font, specify the embedding=true option in the PDF_load_font() function:

```
$font = PDF_load_font($p, "MegaFont", "winansi", "embedding=true");
```

If you omit embedding=true, embedding is disabled by default.

(i)
Embedding PostScript Fonts
To embed a *PostScript* font, include the outlines and metrics of the font. Find the .PFB and .PFA files for the font on the server and include both files in the call to PDF_load_font().

🗗
Code Variation
To load fonts using PDFlib precompiled in PHP 4, use the PDF_findfont() function. The last argument in this functions control embedding. If set to "1" the font is embedded.

```
// PDFlib precompiled with PHP 4 example
$font = PDF_findfont($p, "Helvetica", "host", 1);
```

Font Subsetting

If you use only a handful of characters from a particular or special font (say, a dingbat font), use *font subsetting* to include only those characters you use in the document. Subsetting reduces the size of the generated PDF. (Subsetting may not make a big difference in a small PDF, but if you're creating a large PDF with multiple fonts, subsetting makes very good sense.)

By default, font subsetting is *enabled*, so that a minimum amount of font data is embedded in the PDF. In general, this is desirable, unless you want the user to be able to edit the PDF. (The "Touch-up Tool" in Acrobat won't let a user edit or delete text that uses a subsetted font. However, don't resort to font subsetting as a security measure. Please refer to Chapter 6 to learn how to prevent editing.)

To embed the full character set of all fonts (and thereby enable editing, if necessary), disable font subsetting with the autosubsetting option of PDF_set_paramenter().

```
PDF_set_parameter(p, "autosubsetting", "false");
```

Once (global) subsetting is disabled, you must subset manually if you don't want the entire character set of a font within the PDF. To subset on a case-by-case basis, specify subsetting=true in the PDF_load_font() function:

```
$font = PDF_load_font($p, "MegaFont", "winansi", "embedding=true
subsetting=true");
```

ⓘ **Code Variation**
If you're using PDFlib precompiled with PHP4, enable or disable the auto-subsetting option via PDF_set_parameter().

Controlling the Font

In some circumstances, you may not have the italic or bold versions of a font. Fortunately, PDFlib can artificially create italic and bold variants, if the font you have is a TrueType or OpenType font and you aren't working with one of the core PDF fonts mentioned at the outset.

For example, if you lack the bold variation of the imaginary TrueType font "MegaFont," you can create an artificial "MegaFont-Bold" by setting fontstyle to bold:

```
PDF_load_font(p, "MegaFont", "winansi", "fontstyle=bold");
```

Values for fontstyle include normal, bold, italic, and bolditalic.

Furthermore, to work properly, the encoding of an artificial font must be winansi or macroman, and you cannot embed the artificial font (which implies that the original font has to be present on the viewers machine to allow proper viewing of the artificial font). You can embed the original font, but the font must still reside on the users machine to properly display the artificially created font.

ⓘ **Artificial, Not Official**
An artificial bold or italic font may not have the same visual acuity as the actual bold or italic typeface.

API Exception

The fontstyle option is not available in PDFlib precompiled with PHP4.

Italic Alternative

If you need to italicize a font, use the italicangle option in PDF_set_value().
italicangle skews the font between –12 and –15 degrees, resulting in an italic-
like font, without the restrictions associated with fontstyle. However, the results of italicangle may not be near as good as using an actual italic font.

```
PDF_set_value(p, "italicangle", -15);
PDF_load_font(p, "MegaFont", "winansi", "");
```

API Exception

The italicangle option is not available in PDFlib 5. You must use the font-
sytle variable to achieve this effect.

Overline, Strikeout and Underline

Some circumstances call for text to be overlined, underlined, or struck (which
puts a line through the text). To achieve these effects, use the PDF_set_param-
eter() function and enable one of overline, underline, or strikeout.

For example, the following code creates an overline above the text rendered in MegaFont:

```
PDF_set_parameter(p, "overline", "true");
PDF_load_font(p, "MegaFont", "winansi", "embedding=true");
```

Code Variation

When using PDFlib precompiled with PHP 4, use PDF_set_parameter() followed by PDF_findfont() to create an overline, underline, or strikethrough.

```
// PDFlib precompiled with PHP 4 example
PDF_set_parameter(p, "overline", "true");
PDF_findfont(p, "MegaFont", "winansi", 1);
```

Kerning

Most fonts contain built-in data called *kerning values* that control the space between any pair of characters. For example, without kerning values, an "n" followed by another "n" could be rendered too closely together forming an "m." Kerning values improve the legibility of a font. If you notice strange spacing between characters, enable the kerning option with PDF_set_parameter():

```
PDF_set_parameter(p, "kerning", "true");
```

kerning renders text using the font's prescribed kerning values.

Text Rendering

Almost all of the time, you'll render text as you see it on this page — black, solid characters on a white field. But if you want some special effects, PDFlib allows you to control how text appears. For example, to render only the outline of characters, set the textrendering option to 1 (the numeral one):

```
PDF_set_value(p, "textrendering", 1);
```

You can also render the *clipping path* of text, which is necessary to "reverse out" text on a solid field. A clipping path "clips" or occludes everything rendered below it.

Say you want to print white text over a black box. If you omit the text's clipping path, the printer may simply produce a black box. (The outline of each character in the text is drawn, but it doesn't appear, as it's rendered black on black.) But if you set the render value to 6, which strokes the outline of the font, fills it, and adds the rendered text to the clipping path, the white text appears.

There are eight unique rendering options, enumerated in the table below.

Text Rendering Options	
0	Fill text
1	Stroke text (outline)
2	Fill and stroke text
3	Invisible text
4	Fill text and add it to the clipping path
5	Stroke text and add it to the clipping path
6	Fill and stroke text and add it to the clipping path
7	Add text to the clipping path

Chapter Summary

PDFlib provides tools to accurately control fonts. Used properly, the PDFlib functions create a document that's reproduced accurately across all platforms. To paraphrase "WYSIWYG", "What You See Is What Your (reader) Gets."

5

Using the Block Tool

T HE *PDFLIB* BLOCK TOOL—available for use only with *PDFlib Personalization Server* (PPS)—helps create PDF documents derived from large amounts of variable data.

Before the block tool was added, it was a difficult process to place variable data, images, and even other PDF's into precise areas of a PDF that had been designed previously. Now, adding variable data is very simple and helps create great dynamic pieces for just about any application.

In this chapter, let's discuss the process of combining data from many sources into a single PDF—from installation of the block tool, to creating the blocks in *Adobe Acrobat*, and then finally working with the blocks via PDFlib. Along the way, let's also examine how to set and even override settings that are defined in blocks.

(i) | **The New and Improved Block Tool**
If you've used previous versions of the block tool, you'll notice that the new version is much more user friendly. The export and import features have also been updated, making it much quicker to apply blocks from previously formatted PDFs.

Installing the Block Tool

Currently, the block tool plug-in for *Adobe Acrobat* is only available on the *Windows* and *Macintosh* (both *Mac OS 9* and *Mac OS X)* platforms. On either platform, you must also have *Version 6* or *Version 7* of *Adobe Acrobat Professional* or *Adobe Acrobat Standard,* or the full version of *Adobe Acrobat 5*. As this book went to press, other versions of Adobe Acrobat, *Acrobat Reader,* and *Acrobat Elements,* and all other PDF creation tools do not work with the block tool plug-in. (Check the PDFlib web site for an up-to-date list of supported PDF authoring tools.)

Windows OS Installation

If you're using Windows, you can use the block tool installer provided by PD-Flib to get the plug-in installed correctly into your version of Adobe Acrobat 5, 6, or 7. The installer places the correct files into the Acrobat plug-ins folder, which is typically found at *C:\Program Files\Adobe\Acrobat 6.0\Acrobat\plug_ins\PDFlib*. The Windows version of the block tool is compatible only with *P PS version 6.0.1.*

Mac OS Installation

You can install the block tool in either Mac OS 9 or OS X. If you own Adobe Acrobat 5, place the files that comprise the block tool into the Acrobat plug-in directory, typically located at */Applications/Adobe Acrobat 5.0/Plug-Ins/.*

If you're using Adobe Acrobat version 6 or version 7, save the files that comprise the block tool into a new directory and then locate the Acrobat program, which is usually found */Applications/Adobe Acrobat 6.0 Professional.* Using the *Finder,* click once on the Acrobat application to select it and then choose "File > Get Info" from the menubar. Locate the triangle next to the words "Plug-ins." Expand the triangle, select "Add," and then locate the folder that contains the block tool plug-in files.

(i) **Mac OS X "Tiger"**
If you're using a very recent version of Mac OS X, you can find Acrobat's plug-ins folder by control-clicking the Acrobat application and selecting "Package Content".

Creating Blocks

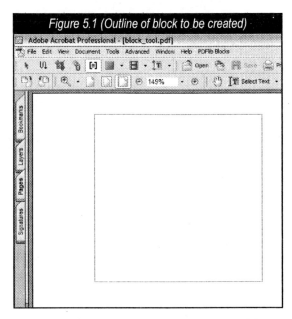

Figure 5.1 (Outline of block to be created)

After you install the block tool, you should see a new menu called "PDFlib Blocks" in Acrobat's main menubar. You should also see a new icon that resembles [=]) — this is the block tool. (See the top of Figure 5.1.) You use the block tool icon to create regions that you can fill with variable data.

When you click the block tool icon and hover over the PDF, your cursor turns into a crosshair. To create a block, click the mouse and hold it as you drag your cursor. As you drag your cursor, a lightly-outlined box should appear. (See *Figure 5.1.*)

When you're satisfied with the size of the box, release the mouse button. A menu like the one shown in *Figure 5.3* appears. The menu con-

Figure 5.2 (Menu for a block created by the block tool)

trols all of the properties of the block, including the formatting of the data that will be contained in the block (data that you will add via PDFlib).

There are three types of blocks that can be created:

Figure 5.3 (A sampling of the text formatting options)

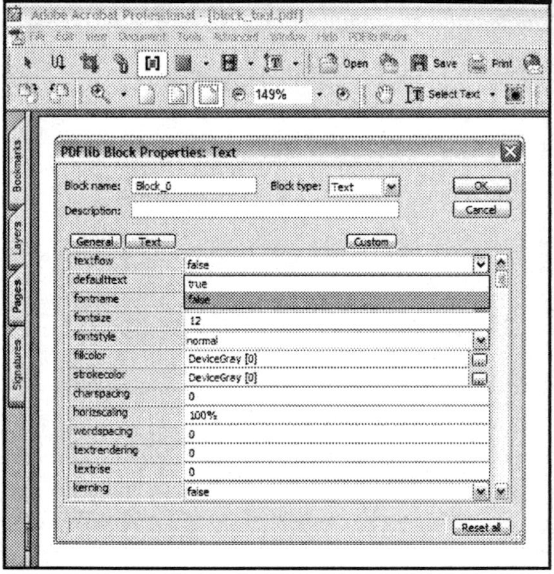

• The first and default type of block is *text*. It handles any type of text, whether it's a single line of text or many lines of text.

• The second type of block is *image*. As its name implies, an image block is a container for the dynamic placement of images within the PDF.

• The third and last type is PDF, which is able to contain other PDFs.

Each block has *general* properties (see *Figure 5.2*) and *type-specific* properties. General properties set attributes such as the placement of the block, its background and border colors, and its orientation, to name just a few. Some of the sections that follow describe the type-specific properties.

So what do you do with blocks? As you might infer already, you use blocks to mix dynamic content amid static content. A designer can create a PDF, include static text and images, and then place blocks wherever dynamic content should appear. You're application "fills in the blanks," so to speak. And because blocks retain properties such as typeface, font size, color, kerning, and other settings, the block, once filled, looks exactly like the rest of document—just as the designer intended.

Using blocks, the application that generates each PDF document need not format anything. However, if you want to customize a block on-the-fly, you can.

Pre-defined block attributes can be overwritten by your code.

Editing Block Settings

To change a block property, select the block you want to configure and then navigate to find the property you want to change. For example, *Figure 5.3* shows how to edit the textflow property, which can be either true or false (hence, the dropdown menu).

The purpose of most properties is obvious, but be careful with attributes that specify font names. Unless you're running Acrobat on the same machine as your PDFlib application, it's likely that the set of fonts on the two machines (say, your desktop and the server, respectively) will differ. Be sure to use the name of fonts that are installed on your *server*.

Form Conversion

You may be familiar with the *Adobe Acrobat* "Form Tool," a great way to create fillable areas of your PDF. So, why not just use forms to define variable data placement? Because the form tool is limited: it cannot specify advanced font settings, whereas the block tool has been designed specifically to customize all aspects of your text. However, if you have a PDF that used the form tool to define areas for text, there is an option within the "PDFlib Blocks" menu to convert your pre-made forms into blocks (*Figure 5.4*).

Text Flow Settings

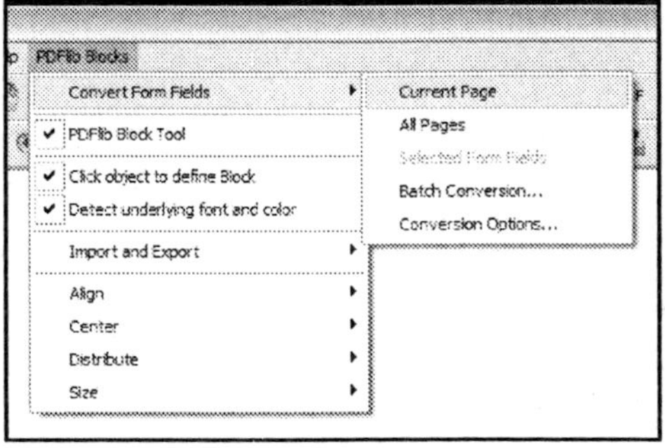

If you want a block to flow (automatically wrap and justify) arbitrary amounts of text, set the textflow property to true. Once set to true, an additional button named *TextFlow* appears next to the existing button labeled *Text*. Click on *TextFlow* to examine and set specific variables (such as leading and indents)

Figure 5.4 (Convert form fields menu)

that control how text flows in the block. All other text attributes—those for one line of text or a flow of text—remain in the same pane as the textflow property.

Image Settings

By changing the block option to *image*, you can use PDFlib to place images dynamically in a PDF. There are far fewer options for an image block than for a text block. The options screen for an image block is shown in *Figure 5.5*.

Figure 5.5 (Image options in the block)

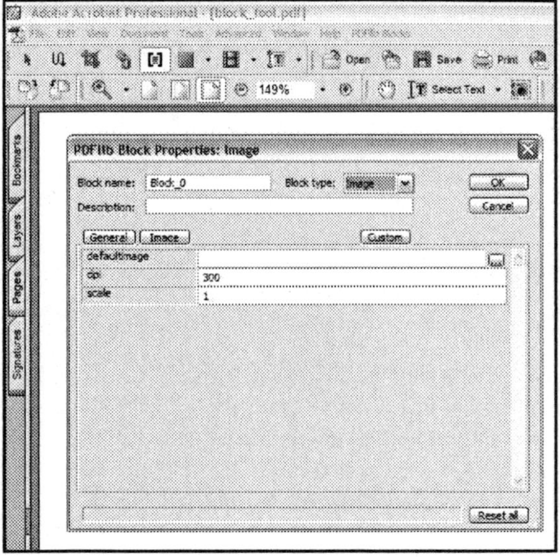

The defaultimage attribute names a default image to place if the image specified by PDFlib is unavailable.

The dpi setting, or the number of dots per inch, is used to override the dpi of an image. PDFlib will use the default dpi value of the image if it is available, or 72 dpi if this option isn't set. If necessary, you can set the horizontal and vertical dpi independently by supplying two values instead of one, first horizontal dpi and then vertical dpi.

The scale property controls the scaling of the image. You can supply one value to scale horizontally and vertically equally, or supply two values, one for the horizontal and another for the vertical scale factor.

PDF Settings

The settings for a *PDF* block are very similar to the settings for an image block, as shown in *Figure 5.6*. defaultpdf specifies a default PDF to place if the PDF document that PDFlib names cannot be found.

defaultpdfpage specifies which page of the default PDF to place if the default PDF must be used.

scale controls the scaling of the PDF. As with an image, you can specify one value to apply to both axes or you can provide two values, one for horizontal scaling and another for vertical scaling.

Custom Settings

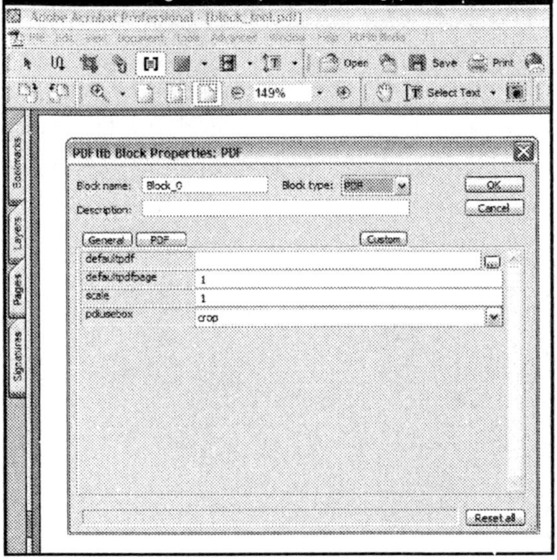

When using any type of block, you can specify *custom attributes*. Custom attributes *do not* affect the output when using PDFlib, but can be retrieved by PDFlib for interpretation by your code. Custom attributes are good for passing information to the PDFlib program, or even for just better record keeping. As an example, say that you want to create a text block that's limited to ten

Figure 5.6 (PDF Settings)

characters or less. Create the text block, add a custom property named length, set it to 10, and then retrieve the value via PDFlib at runtime. Your code can verify the length of a string before filling the block and react accordingly, perhaps truncating the string or asking the user to provide a new value.

The PDFlib Blocks Menu

To make setting up blocks easier, the "PDFlib Blocks" menu has a few handy tools. You can export and import blocks to re-use complex blocks, you can align elements, and more.

Exporting

The "Export" feature is a huge timesaver when dealing with multiple PDFs that require the same types of blocks. Once you've finished setting up blocks in a single "master" PDF, you can export those blocks and then import them over and over again into other PDFs. There are several different settings in the "Export" dialog (see Figure 5.7):

Figure 5.7 (Export Block options)

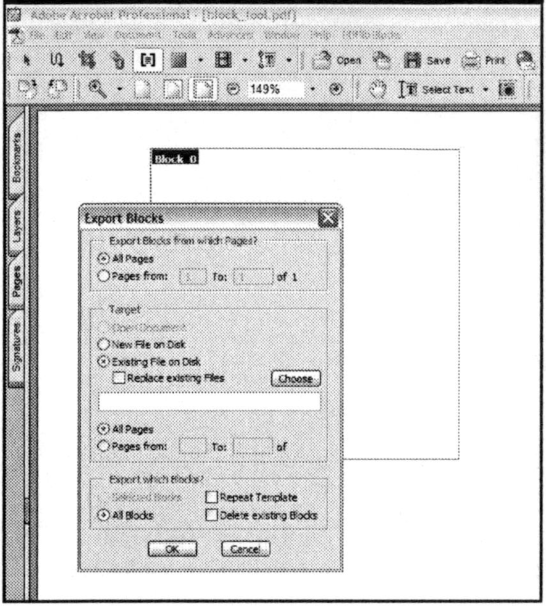

• You can export blocks from all pages of the PDF or from a subset of them.

• You can export blocks to a new PDF or to an existing PDF. Selecting "New File on Disk" creates a blank PDF with the blocks set in the new file. If you want to export blocks to a document that you already have opened in Adobe Acrobat, select "Open Document" and click "Choose" to see a list of all open documents. If you choose "Replace Existing Files", the block tool will overwrite the target file with blank pages with the blocks in the proper place.

• The next option is "Export Which Blocks?" This section allows you to conztrol which blocks are exported. You can export all blocks—depending on the amount of pages you choose in the first section—or just the blocks that you highlight before exporting. You can also choose to delete the blocks that exist on the target PDF.

Importing

You can import blocks from another PDF using the import option in the "PD-Flib Blocks" menu. When you choose "Import," you will be presented with a screen to choose the file that contains the blocks you want to import (*Figure 5.8*).

After you choose the appropriate file, you can determine which pages the blocks should be applied to.

Alignment Options

The alignment option in the "PDFlib Blocks" menu allows you to align two blocks.

To align, choose a block. It should turn pink, reflecting that it's your primary choice. Then choose another block; it should turn blue, indicating that its your secondary choice. When you select "Align", the blue block should align with the pink block. *Figure 5.9* shows two blocks, Block_1, the secondary block, left-aligned to the primary block, Block_0.

The "Size" alignment option only works when more than one block is selected. You can change all secondary blocks (blue) to be either the same width or height as the primary block (pink).

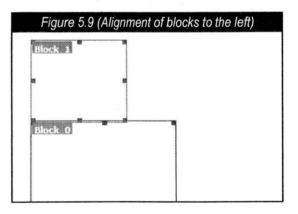

Figure 5.8 (Import block options)

Figure 5.9 (Alignment of blocks to the left)

The "Center" alignment option aligns all blocks selected either horizontally or vertically, and even both horizontally and vertically.

Defining Blocks and Detecting Settings

Two other time savers are available in the "PDFlib Block" menu: one creates a block from a placed object like an image, and another creates blocks that automatically detect the font settings and font color of the font that the block is being created *over*.

Click on "Click Object to Define Block" and then click on an object such as an image to create a block of the same dimension in the exact same position.

Or, if you click on "Detect Underlying Font and Color" before you create a block, the the block's font settings are automatically set to match the style and size of the text below the new block. This feature is especially useful when dealing with a lot of text and specific colors. (You may have to adjust the font name to match a font located on the server running PDFlib.)

Using Blocks

As you might imagine, working with blocks from within your code makes placing text, images, and PDFs into a dynamic PDF far simpler than writing code to control the pointer, stroke text line-by-line, and so on. With blocks, formatting is separated from your code, leaving all of the aesthetics to the designer creating the PDF. Better yet, a change to the design of the page doesn't (necessarily) necessitate tweaking your code.

Setting up the dynamic PDF document is similar to what's been shown in prior chapters, except you need to pull in the PDF that contains the blocks. First, specify the basic information:

```
if (!extension_loaded('pdf')) {
dl('libpdf_php.so');
}

$p = PDF_new();

PDF_begin_document($p, "", "");

PDF_set_info($p, "Creator", "block_tool.php");
PDF_set_info($p, "Author", "Ron Goff");
PDF_set_info($p, "Title", "Block Tool");
```

Next, pull in the PDF page that contains the blocks, place it into memory, and create a new blank page:

```
$block_file = "block_file.pdf";
$blockcontainer = PDF_open_pdi($p, $block_file, "", 0);
```

```
//Page standard 8.5 x 11
PDF_begin_page_ext($p, 612, 792, "");
```

Continuing, call up the actual page that you want to use. In the line of code below, the 1 (numeral one) refers to page one of the PDF that contains the blocks.

```
$page = PDF_open_pdi_page($p, $blockcontainer, 1, "");
```

If you want to use another page from the "template" PDF, just specify that page number instead of 1.

Finally, the page with blocks is "copied" to the new page in the new PDF.

```
PDF_fit_pdi_page($p, $page, 0.0, 0.0, "adjustpage");
```

The option adjustpage adjusts the size of the new page to match the page size of the template PDF. adjustpage overrides any page settings that have been set previously.

From here, you are ready to use the blocks.

Text Blocks

Whether working with a line of text or a text flow, text flows are easy to fill in: just specify the name of the block and the text to render and call PDF_fill_text-block().

```
$block = "Block_1";
$text = "All the pie in the sky wasn't enough to fill my plate";
PDF_fill_textblock($p, $page, $block, $text, "encoding=winansi");
```

The block name, here Block_1, is the name that was assigned to the block when it was created in the template PDF. (Block names are unique and the default name is Block_#, but a block name can be any string of alphanumeric characters.)

Notice that there are no extra formatting options. Whatever text you "insert" assumes the formatting of the block.

If you want to override a block's formatting, you can. Where encoding=winansi appears, add the options that you want to override. For example, to override the font size, specify encoding=winansi fontsize=12.

You should also enable embedding as needed. You can enable embedding by adding embedding=true as in encoding=winansi embedding=true.

Image Blocks

The process of placing an image in an image block resembles that of placing the image "manually": the image is loaded and then placed.

```
$block4 = "Block_4";
$image_load = "image.jpg";
$image = PDF_load_image($p, "auto", $image_load, "");
PDF_fill_imageblock($p, $page, $block4, $image, "");
PDF_close_image($p, $image);
```

In this example, the image image.jpg is placed in Block_4 using the function PDF_fill_imageblock().

PDF Blocks

The steps to place a PDF document within the dynamically-generated PDF are similar to the steps required to set up a page to work with blocks. You identify what block you want to "fill," identify the PDF and the page you want to extract from, and then fill the named block with that content.

```
$block5 = "Block_5";
$pdf_load = "basic_pdf.pdf";
$pdf = PDF_open_pdi($p, $pdf_load, "", 0);
$pdf_fill = PDF_open_pdi_page($p, $pdf, 1, "");
```

```
PDF_fill_pdfblock($p, $page, $block5, $pdf_fill, "");
PDF_close_pdi($p, $pdf);
```

PDF_open_pdi() opens the PDF, while PDF_open_pdi_page() loads the correct page. The function PDF_fill_pdfblock() puts it all together, placing the actual PDF onto the page. Finally, close the open PDF by calling PDF_close_pdi(), which frees the resources consumed by the open PDF.

Closing the Page

After you've filled all of the appropriate blocks on the open page, you must close that page.

```
PDF_close_pdi_page($p, $page);
```

This line closes the PDF and you can start a new page, or end the entire document after this is called.

Putting It All Together

Here is a complete example using the PDF_fill_textblock() function.

```php
<?php
if (!extension_loaded('pdf')) {
  dl('libpdf_php.so');
}

$p = PDF_new();
PDF_begin_document($p, "", "");

PDF_set_info($p, "Creator", "block_tool.php");
PDF_set_info($p, "Author", "Ron Goff");
PDF_set_info($p, "Title", "Block Tool");

$block_file = "block_file.pdf";

$blockcontainer = PDF_open_pdi($p, $block_file, "", 0);

PDF_begin_page_ext($p, 612, 792, "");

$page = PDF_open_pdi_page($p, $blockcontainer, 1, "");
```

```
PDF_fit_pdi_page($p, $page, 0.0, 0.0, "adjustpage");

$block = "Block_1";
$text = "All the pie in the sky wasn't enough to fill my plate";
PDF_fill_textblock($p, $page, $block, $text, "");

PDF_close_pdi($p, $blockcontainer);

PDF_close_pdi_page($p, $page);
PDF_end_page_ext($p, "");
PDF_end_document($p, "");

$buf = PDF_get_buffer($p);
$len = strlen($buf);

header("Content-type: application/pdf");
header("Content-Length: $len");
header("Content-Disposition: inline; filename=block_pdf.pdf");
print $buf;

PDF_delete($p);
?>
```

Chapter Summary

The PDFlib block tool is easy-to-use and provides for complex layouts without extensive programming. Using blocks, a designer can assign where dynamic text, images, and even PDFs are to be placed, yielding a much more professional result.

6

Optimization, Security & Compatibility

IN ADDITION TO CONTROLLING THE CONTENT OF A PDF, you can also control how a PDF is viewed. If your PDF is large, you may choose to optimize the document to be delivered in stages, which prevents the interminable wait (however real or perceived) as the file is transmitted from server to browser. In some instances, you may want to secure a PDF with a password, so only your intended recipient can read it. Or perhaps your PDF is highly specialized and depends on a certain class of PDF reader to display properly. Optimization, security, and compatibility can all be tuned via *PDFlib*.

Optimizing Your PDF

Linearization, also known as *optimization* or *fast Web view*, allows you to "stream" a PDF to your end-user. Rather than wait until the entire document is downloaded, optimization displays what's been downloaded as soon as possible. As soon as the first page of a PDF has been downloaded, it's displayed immediately. Meanwhile, the second page is downloaded, and so on.

If you're rendering something like an online PDF magazine or an entire PDF book—documents that are fairly large—optimization makes downloads seem faster, sparing the user from watching an hourglass spin and spin.

By default, optimization is disabled. However, it's simple to optimize your PDF: just set `linearize=true` in the `PDF_begin_document()` function.

```
PDF_begin_document($p, "", "linearize=true");
```

Code Variant

Unfortunately, optimization isn't available in PDFlib 5 or in the version of PDFlib that comes precompiled with PHP4.

The creation of a linearized PDF is a two-stage process: first, a normal unoptimized PDF is created; next, it's optimized. By default, both documents are stored temporarily on the filesystem of the PDF-generating server. You can, however, keep the entire optimization process in memory, gaining some performance (albeit at the expense of consuming extra memory). To optimize in memory, set `linearize=true` and set `inmemory=true` true in `PDF_begin_document()`.

```
PDF_begin_document($p, "", "inmemory=true linearize=true");
```

If you fail to set `linearize=true`, `inmemory=true` is ineffectual.

Password Protection

Occasionally or depending on your type of pursuit, you may need to apply a password to a PDF and set permissions to hinder the editing or printing of the PDF by the end-user. PDFlib allows you to set a master password, a user password, and various access permissions to help secure a PDF.

Encrypted PDFs
Anytime a password is set, the PDF is encrypted, using either 40-bit or 128-bit keys, depending on the compatibility version you specify (see the next section). When an encrypted PDF is viewed in a reader like *Adobe Acrobat Reader 6.0,* a lock icon will be shown in the lower left corner. Right click on that icon to see the security and permission settings and the encryption strength.

Setting the Master Password

A PDF master password is used to configure security settings and access permissions, and to enable the use of a user password. If only the master password is set, the PDF can be viewed freely by any end-user. However, if the master password is set, it must be provided to make changes to the PDF's security settings and access permissions.

To set the master password, place the master password after the master-password option in the PDF_beging_document() function.

```
PDF_begin_document($p, "", "masterpassword=mp324");
```

The master password must be present to set the permissions of a PDF and to set the user password.

Code Variation
Passwords are handled slightly differently in *PDFlib version 5* and *PDFlib* precompiled with *PHP4.* Use the function PDF_set_parameter() *after* the PDF_new() function.

```
// PDFlib5 or PDFlib precompiled with PHP 4 example
$p = PDF_new();
PDF_set_parameter($p, "masterpassword", "mp324");
```

Setting the User Password

If you want to limit who can view a PDF, supply a user password. To set the user password, use the "userpassword" option in the PDF_begin_document() function.

```
PDF_begin_document($p, "", "masterpassword=mp324
userpassword=u432");
```

The user password may not be the same phrase as the master password.

Code Variation

If you're using PDFlib version 5 or PDFlib precompiled with PHP4, use the function PDF_set_parameter() to set the user password *after* you set the master password.

```
// PDFlib precompiled with PHP 4 example
$p = PDF_new();
PDF_set_parameter($p, "masterpassword", "mp324");
PDF_set_parameter($p, "userpassword", "u432");
```

Using Permissions

Permissions control what can be done with a PDF. You must at least set the master password to enable permissions.

There are several access rights available and you can use any combination of them in a PDF. (However, some of the settings are only available in newer versions of PDF.) For example, the following code disables the ability to print the PDF (unless the master password is provided and printing is re-enabled).

```
PDF_begin_document($p, "", "masterpassword=mp324
permissions={noprint}");
```

Put your permissions options after the master password.

Code Variation

When using PDFlib 5 or PDFlib precompiled with PHP4, set permissions of the PDF in the PDF_set_parameter() after the master password is set.

```
// PDFlib5 or PDFlib precompiled with PHP 4 example
$p = PDF_new();
PDF_set_parameter($p, "masterpassword", "mp324");
PDF_set_parameter($p, "permissions", "noprint");
```

These are all the available permissions:

- noaccessible disables the ability to extract text or graphics to be used in accessibility programs. (Requires Adobe Acrobat 5.0+ compatibility.)

- noannots disables the ability to add and edit comments and form fields.

- noassemble disables the ability to insert and delete pages, rotate pages, and create bookmarks and thumbnails. (Requires Adobe Acrobat 5.0+ compatibility.)

- nocopy disables the ability to copy any of the text or graphics.

- noforms disables the filling of form fields. (Requires Adobe Acrobat 5.0+ compatibility.)

- nohiresprint disables the ability to print the PDF in high-resolution. (Requires Adobe Acrobat 5.0+ compatibility.)

- nomodify disables any editing of the PDF.

- noprint disables the ability to print the PDF.

- plainmetadata presents the PDF file metadata plainly even if the PDF has been encrypted. (Requires Adobe Acrobat 6.0+ compatibility. This option is not available to PDFlib version 5 or PDFlib precompiled with PHP4.)

Using a Protected PDF

Infrequently, you may need to use a PDF with PDFlib that's been password protected. To use or import a protected PDF, you must pass along the appropriate *master* password. To set the master password to import a PDF, set the password option in the PDF_open_pdi() function:

```
PDF_open_pdi($p, $block_file, "password=mp324", 0);
```

If you don't need to import a password-protected PDF, but just need its blocks, use the infomode=true option. infomode=true bypasses the need to supply the master password.

```
PDF_open_pdi($p, $pdf_file, "infomode=true", 0);
```

However, if the password-protected PDF has a user password, you must supply that password with password along with the infomode option itself, as in:

```
PDF_open_pdi($p, $pdf_file, "infomode=true password=u432", 0);
```

Code Variation
The infomode option is not available to those using PDFlib 5 or PDFlib pre-compiled with PHP4.

Compatibility

There are a large number of PDF viewers available, and capabilities from one viewer to another can and do differ. If you depend on a certain PDF feature, set the compatibility mode appropriately to ensure that your documents are viewed in a suitable viewer. For example, if the PDF files you're generating use a feature introduced in Acrobat version 7.0, set the compatibility mode to version 1.6.

ⓘ | **PDF Versions**
Some PDF documents are so simple that all PDF viewers can open and display the content regardless of the compatibility mode. However, those PDF documents that depend on recently-introduced features may not display correctly in older PDF readers. In fact, in some cases, older readers may not be able to open such a PDF.

To set the compatibility level, set the compatibility option to the PDF version your documents depend on in the PDF_begin_document() function:

```
PDF_begin_document($p, "", "compatibility=1.6");
```

The line of code above sets the PDF to be compatible with Adobe Acrobat versions 7.0 and above.

| **Code Variation**
If you're coding with PDFlib 5 or PDFlib precompiled with PHP 4, set the compatibility mode with the PDF_set_parameter() function.

```
// PDFlib5 or PDFlib precompiled with PHP 4 example
PDF_set_parameter($p, "compatibility", "1.5");
```

For your reference, certain versions of the PDF specifications correspond to versions of Adobe Acrobat.

PDF Ver.	Adobe Acrobat Ver.
1.3	4.0
1.4	5.0
1.5	6.0
1.6	7.0*

As mentioned previously, the PDF version you choose also affects the level of encryption. All PDF versions 1.3 (Adobe Acrobat 4) and below utilize 40-bit encryption, which is not very strong. This is something you may want to consider when setting compatibility.

Not available with PDFlib 5 or PDFlib precompiled with PHP 4.

Chapter Summary

Via PDFlib, you can control how your PDF is downloaded, can control who can access your PDF, and can control what an end-user can do with your document. Moreover, if you depend on a certain feature found in a revision of the PDF specification, you can set the compatibility mode in your document to limit viewing to capable software.

7
Practical
Applications

L ET'S TAKE A LOOK at a few practical applications of *PDFlib* to spark further ideas and demonstrate some of the ways that PDFlib can fit into a workflow.

Create a Dynamic Memo

This example uses PDFlib to create a simple memo. The text of the memo could come from a database or from an incoming email message. You can find the code for this example in the file *prac_app_1.php*. This example works with PD-Flib precompiled with PHP4, *PDFlib 5*, and *PDFlib 6*.

First, create a new PDF using the same code shown in previous chapters:

```
<?php
if (!extension_loaded('pdf')) {
  dl("libpdf_php.so")
}
$p = PDF_new();
```

Next, create (or extract or lookup) the actual content of the memo. For simplicity, this code just sets a handful of variables to strings, but the content could just as easily have been parsed from an email message or loaded from a *MySQL* database.

```
$from_db = "Ronald Goff";
$to_db = "Staff";
$phone_db = "(555) 555-5555";

$text_db = "I would like to inform the staff that lunches will now
feature the spork. To cut cost we have decided to replace the spoon
and fork with this ingenious product.";
```

The next section of code begins the page. The page size is the standard 8.5" x 11".

```
PDF_begin_document($p, "", "");
PDF_set_info($p, "Creator", "prac_app_1.php");
PDF_set_info($p, "Author", "Ron Goff");
PDF_set_info($p, "Title", "Dynamic Memo PDF");
PDF_begin_page_ext($p, 612, 792, "");
```

Next, the core font "Helvetica-Bold" is loaded. It will be reused in several places in a variety of point sizes.

```
$font = PDF_load_font($p, "Helvetica-Bold", "winansi", "");
PDF_setfont($p, $font, 45);
```

Continuing, black is chosen as the default color, because the memo is to be printed on a black-and-white printer.

```
PDF_setcolor($p, "both", "rgb", 0, 0, 0, 0);
```

With basic configuration out of the way, the title of the memo is printed in a large font at the top of the page:

```
PDF_set_text_pos($p, 10, 700);
PDF_show($p, "MEMO");
```

Next, the code creates a long black rectangle right below the title.

```
PDF_setlinewidth($p, ".52");
PDF_moveto($p,10,690);
PDF_lineto($p,602,690);
PDF_lineto($p,602,680);
PDF_lineto($p,10,680);
PDF_fill($p);
```

This next section of code creates the "To" and "From" parts of the memo. The text is printed in 70 percent black, a dark grey color.

```
PDF_fit_textline($p, "From: $from_db", 10,  650, "fillcolor={rgb .7
.7 .7} fontsize=20");
PDF_fit_textline($p, "To: $to_db", 10,  620, "fillcolor={rgb .7 .7
.7} fontsize=20");
```

A text flow box is used for the body of the memo. The body of the memo is rendered in Helvetica.

```
$textbox = PDF_create_textflow($p, $text_db, "alignment=left
leading=100% fontname=Helvetica fontsize=12
fillcolor={rgb 0 0 0} encoding=winansi");

PDF_fit_textflow($p, $textbox, 10, 600, 602, 150, "");
PDF_delete_textflow($p, $textbox);
```

Since Helvetica-Bold (used earlier) and Helvetica (used immediately above) are core fonts, there's no need to embed the fonts in the document.

The next section of code prints the name of the person sending the memo and his or her phone number, which concludes the text that's printed on the PDF. The font size changes twice, once for the name and again for the phone number.

```
PDF_setfont($p, $font, 15);
PDF_set_text_pos($p, 10, 75);
PDF_show($p, "$from_db");

PDF_setfont($p, $font, 10);
PDF_set_text_pos($p, 10, 60);
PDF_show($p, "$phone_db");
```

Finally, the PDF page is closed, the document is closed, and the result is sent to the screen.

```
PDF_end_page_ext($p, "");
PDF_end_document($p, "");

$buf = PDF_get_buffer($p);
$len = strlen($buf);

header("Content-type: application/pdf");
header("Content-Length: $len");
header("Content-Disposition: inline; filename=memo.pdf");
print $buf;

PDF_delete($p);
?>
```

The end-result looks something like Figure 7.1.

Although the memo example is very simple, it shows several combinations for displaying text, setting fonts, and setting font colors in a single PDF.

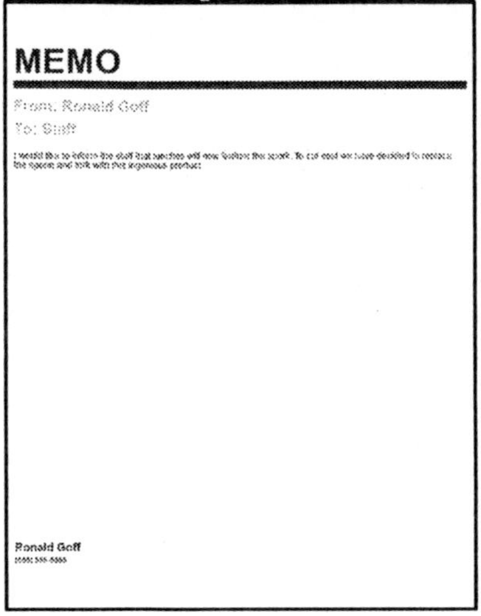

Figure 7.1

Merging PDF Documents

As a slightly more complex example, let's take an array of PDF file names and merge the set of files into one PDF. To be able to import and use other PDFs, you must use the abilities of *PDFlib PDI* or *PDFlib PPS*. You can find the code for this example in *prac_app_2.php*.

Again, start off with the standard way of creating a PDF with PDFlib:

```php
<?php
if (!extension_loaded('pdf')) {
  dl("libpdf_php.so")
}

$p = PDF_new();

PDF_begin_document($p, "", "");

PDF_set_info($p, "Creator", "prac_app_2.php");
PDF_set_info($p, "Author", "Ron Goff");
PDF_set_info($p, "Title", "Merging Documents");
```

$doc_holder is the array of file names to import and merge. The code iterates over the array, opening each PDF file.

```
$doc_holder = array("Merge_Doc_1.pdf", "Merge_Doc_2.pdf");
foreach($doc_holder as $merg_doc){
   // begin document loop
   $merge_container = PDF_open_pdi($p, $merg_doc, "", 0);
```

The PDF_get_pdi_value() function can extract specific information from an opened PDF. Here, the code extracts how many pages are in the PDF that was just opened. The number of pages is captured in $count_pages.

```
$count_pages = PDF_get_pdi_value($p, "/Root/Pages/Count", $merge_
container, 0, 0);
```

The next loop creates a new blank page in the new PDF for every page in the PDF to be merged. Once each new page is created, the corresponding existing PDF page is copied to the new document and both pages are closed.

```
if($counter == ''){
$counter = 1;
}

while($counter <= $count_pages){
   PDF_begin_page_ext($p, 612, 792, "");
   $page = PDF_open_pdi_page($p, "$merge_container", $counter, "");
   PDF_fit_pdi_page($p, $page, 0.0, 0.0, "");
   PDF_close_pdi_page($p, $page);
   PDF_end_page_ext($p, "");
```

When the last page of each existing PDF document is reached, the counter is reset and the next PDF in the array $doc_holder is processed.

```
    $counter++;
}

unset($counter);
}
```

Once all of the documents in doc_holder are processed, the merge is complete. The new document is closed and then emitted to the screen.

```
PDF_end_document($p, "");

$buf = PDF_get_buffer($p);
$len = strlen($buf);

header("Content-type: application/pdf");
header("Content-Length: $len");
header("Content-Disposition: inline; filename=merge_pdf.pdf");
print $buf;

PDF_delete($p);
?>
```

Creating an Image Index

In this example, let's create an image index of the cover art of past issues of *PHP|Architect* magazine. Here, let's use a PDF that includes image blocks created with the *PDFlib Block Tool* in *Adobe Acrobat*. The blocks have been defined to automatically scale down an image to fit the box, if necessary. You can find the code for this example in *prac_app_3.php*. This example *requires* PDFlib PPS.

This preamble should look familiar by now:

```
<?php
if (!extension_loaded('pdf')) {
dl("libpdf_php.so")
}

$p = PDF_new();
```

```
PDF_begin_document($p, "", "");

PDF_set_info($p, "Creator", "prac_app_3.php");
PDF_set_info($p, "Author", "Ron Goff");
PDF_set_info($p, "Title", "Cover Index PDF");
```

The next step is to open the PDF that contains the image blocks and place it in memory for later use.

```
$block_file = "cover_file.pdf";
$blockcontainer = PDF_open_pdi($p, $block_file, "", 0);
```

To continue, create a new page and place the necessary page from the "template" PDF—in this case, page 1—onto a blank page.

```
PDF_begin_page_ext($p, 612, 792, "");

$page = PDF_open_pdi_page($p, $blockcontainer, 1, "");

PDF_fit_pdi_page($p, $page, 0.0, 0.0, "");
```

The next two lines of code initialize a counter, $block_num and an arrary, $mag_covers. The counter controls which block to place an image into. The array corresponds to numbers found in the title of the magazine cover images.

```
$block_num = 1;
$mag_covers = array("47", "45", "44", "42", "40", "36", "34", "32",
"30", "28", "26", "24");
```

The work of this application is to iterate over the covers, loading each cover and placing it into its corresponding block. PDF_fill_imageblock() places each image into its box.

```
foreach($mag_covers as $mag){
$block = "Block_".$block_num;
$image_pre = "images/mag".$mag.".jpg";

$image = PDF_load_image($p, "auto", $image_pre, "");
PDF_fill_imageblock($p, $page, $block, $image, "");
$block_num++;
}
```

Remember that the size of each image is irrelevant, because each block has been configured to automatically fit its image to its own extents.

Finally, close the PDF that contains the blocks, end the new page just created. close the new document, and send it to the screen.

```
PDF_close_pdi_page($p, $page);
PDF_end_page_ext($p, "");
PDF_end_document($p, "");

$buf = PDF_get_buffer($p);
$len = strlen($buf);

header("Content-type: application/pdf");
header("Content-Length: $len");
header("Content-Disposition: inline; filename=hello.pdf");
print $buf;

PDF_delete($p);
?>
```

The image index example will look something like Figure 7.2 (next page).

An image index can be used in several different ways. You could use the index to create a dynamic layout of classified ads, for example. Instead of placing each ad by hand, you would merely set up a template and reference the images. Alternately, by converting the blocks on the template PDF to accept other PDFs, you could import PDFs of the classified ads directly into the template.

Chapter Summary

There are so many ways to use PDFlib—these examples show the very tip of a gigantic iceberg.

Figure 7.2

Appendix

PDF_add_bookmark($p, *text, parent, open*)

This function creates a bookmark in a PDF.   ·PDFlib 5, PHP4

Text	STRING	The title of the bookmark. Maximum length is 255 characters but 32 characters are suggested.
Parent	0	The bookmark will become a parent.
Parent	1	The bookmark will be nested under the first parent bookmark.
Open	0	The bookmarks children will be collapsed.
Open	1	The bookmarks children will be shown. (This is optional in the version of PDFlib precompiled with PHP4)

This function will work with PDFlib 5 and PDFlib precompiled with PHP4. It has been replaced in PDFlib 6 with PDF_create_bookmark().

PDF_attach_file ($p, llx, lly, urx, ury, filename, description, author, mimetype, icon)

This function will attach a file onto a PDF.   PDFlib 5, PHP4

Llx	The lower left x position.
Lly	The lower left y position.
Urx	The upper right x position.
Ury	The upper right y position.
Filename	Set the name of the file that will be attached.
Description	The description of the file that is attached.
Author	The author and person attaching the file.
Mimetype	Properly sets the mime type for attaching the file.
Icon	Specifies which icon is to be used that will be visible on the PDF.

This function will work with PDFlib 5 and PDFlib precompiled with PHP4. It has been replaced in PDFlib 6 with PDF_create_annotation().

PDF_begin_document($p, "filename", "options")

This function begins a new PDF document.   PDFlib 6, PHP5

Filename	If this option has been set with a filename the document will be created on disk. If the filename is not given the document will be created in memory.
Options	Options can be set to control several aspects of the created PDF.

compatibility	[1.3, 1.4, 1.5, 1.6]
inmemory	[true, false]
linerize	[true, false]
masterpassword	string of characters
userpassword	string of characters

This function will work with PDFlib 6 and PDFlib precompiled with PHP5. For those using PDFlib 5 or PDFlib precompiled with PHP4 you will use the PDF_open_file() function.

PDF_begin_page($p, width, height)

This function starts a new page in the document.　　　PDFlib 5, PHP4

Width	The width of the page in points.
Height	The height of the page in points.

This function will work with PDFlib 5 and PDFlib precompiled with PHP4. It has been replaced in PDFlib 6 with PDF_begin_page_ext().

PDF_begin_page_ext($p, width, height, "options")

This function starts a new page in the document.　　　PDFlib 6, PHP5

Width	The width of the page in points.
Height	The height of the page in points.
Options	Options can be set to control several aspects of the new page.

Sample page sizes in inches converted to points:

8.5 x 11 (Letter)	=	612 x 792	A3	=	842 X 1190
8.5 x 14 (Legal)	=	612 x 1008	A4	=	595 x 842
11 x 17 (Ledger)	=	792 x 1224	A5	=	421 x 595
A0	=	2380 x 3368	A6	=	297 x 421
A1	=	1684 x 2380	B5	=	501 x 709
A2	=	1190 X 1684			

This function will work with PDFlib 6 and PDFlib precompiled with PHP5. For those using PDFlib 5 or PDFlib precompiled with PHP4 you will use the PDF_begin_page() *function.*

PDF_circle($p, x, y, radius)

This function creates a circle.　　　PDFlib 5, PDFlib 6, PHP4, PHP5

X	The x center position on the page.
Y	The y center position on the page.
Radius	The radius of the circle.

This function will work with PDFlib 5, PDFlib 6, PDFlib precompiled with PHP4 and PDFlib precompiled with PHP5.

PDF_close(p)

This function closes a PDF that is created with
PDF_open_file().

PDFlib 5, PHP4

This function will work with PDFlib5 and PDFlib precompiled with PHP4. It has been replaced in PDFlib 6 with PDF_end_document().

PDF_close_image(p, *image handle*)

This function closes an image that was opened PDF_load_image().

PDFlib 5, PDFlib 6, PHP4, PHP5

Image handle	The image handle created by the function PDF_load_image().

This function will work with PDFlib 5, PDFlib 6, PDFlib precompiled with PHP4 and PDFlib precompiled with PHP5.

PDF_close_pdi_page(p, *page handle*)

This function closes a PDF opened by PDF_open_pdi_page().

PDFlib 5 PDI or PPS, PDFlib 6 PDI or PPS

Page handle	The PDF handle created by the function PDF_open_pdi_page().

This function will only work with PDFlib 5 PDI or PPS and PDFlib 6 PDI or PPS.

PDF_continue_text(p, *"text"*)

This function will continue the text onto a new line after PDF_show_xy(), PDF_set_text_pos(), or PDF_show_text_boxed().

PDFlib 5, PDFlib 6, PHP4, PHP5

Text	A string of text to be placed onto the page.

This function will work with PDFlib 5, PDFlib 6, PDFlib precompiled with PHP4 and PDFlib precompiled with PHP5.

PDF_create_annotation (p, *llx, lly, urx, ury, "type", "options"*)

This function will create annotation onto a PDF.

PDFlib6, PHP5

Llx	The lower left x position.

Lly	The lower left y position.
Urx	The upper right x position.
Ury	The upper right y position.
Type	This indicates the type of annotation to be made.
Options	Options can be set to control several aspects of the annotation.

This function will work with PDFlib 6 and PDFlib precompiled with PHP5. For those using PDFlib 5 or PDFlib precompiled with PHP4 you will use the PDF_attach _file() *function.*

PDF_create_bookmark($p, *"text", "options"*)

This function creates a bookmark in a PDF.   PDFlib 6, PHP5

Text	The title of the bookmark. A maximum of 32 characters is suggested.	
Options	Options can be set to control several aspects of the created bookmark.	
	open=false	The bookmarks children will be collapsed.
	open=true	The bookmarks children will be shown.
	parent=0	The bookmark will become a parent.*
	parent=1	The bookmark will be nested under the first bookmark.*
	* You can continue the number series to create nested bookmarks.	

This function will work with PDFlib 6 and PDFlib precompiled with PHP5. For those using PDFlib 5 or PDFlib precompiled with PHP4 you will use the PDF_add_bookmark() *function.*

PDF_create_textflow($p, *"text", "options"*)

This function will preprocess the text that will be later used with PDF_fit_textflow().   PDFlib 6, PHP5

Text	A string of text to be placed into a texflow object.
Options	options can be set to control several aspects of the created texflow.

alignment	[Left, right, center, justify]
leading	Number or percentage.
fontsize	Number representing size of font.
fillcolor	Color of text. Example: fillcolor={rgb 0 0 0}
encoding	The text encoding.

This function will work with PDFlib 6 and PDFlib precompiled with PHP5.

PDF_delete($p)

This function deletes a PDFlib object and will free all resources used by the object.

PDFlib 5, PDFlib 6, PHP4, PHP5

This function will work with PDFlib 5, PDFlib 6, PDFlib precompiled with PHP4 and PDFlib precompiled with PHP5.

PDF_delete_textflow($p, textflow handle)

This function deletes a textflow.

PDFlib 6, PHP5

Textflow handle	A textflow handle created by PDF_create_textflow().

This function will work with PDFlib 6 and PDFlib precompiled with PHP5.

PDF_end_document($p, "options")

This function closes a PDF that is created with PDF_begin_document().

PDFlib 6, PHP5

Options	Options can be set to control several aspects of the created PDF. Options set here will replace options set in PDF_begin_document().	
	compatibility	[1.3, 1.4, 1.5, 1.6]
	inmemory	[true, false]
	linerize	[true, false]
	masterpassword	string of characters
	userpassword	string of characters

This function will work with PDFlib 6 and PDFlib precompiled with PHP5. For those using PDFlib 5 or PDFlib precompiled with PHP4 you will use the PDF_close() function.

PDF_end_page(p)

This function closes a page created by PDF_begin_page(). ■ PDFlib 5, PHP4

This function will work with PDFlib 5 and PDFlib precompiled with PHP4. It has been replaced in PDFlib 6 with PDF_end_page_ext().

PDF_end_page_ext(p, "options")

This function closes a page created by PDF_begin_page_ext(). ■ PDFlib 6, PHP5

Options	options can be set to control several aspects of the created page. Options set here will replace options set in PDF_begin_page().

This function will work with PDFlib 6 and PDFlib precompiled with PHP5. For those using PDFlib 5 or PDFlib precompiled with PHP4 you will use the PDF_end_page() function.

PDF_fill(p)

This function fills the current path with a fill color. ■ PDFlib 5, PDFlib 6, PHP4, PHP5

This functions could be replaced by PDF_fill_stroke() for filling and outlining path and PDF_stroke() for outlining path. This function will work with PDFlib 5, PDFlib 6, PDFlib precompiled with PHP4 and PDFlib precompiled with PHP5.

PDF_fill_textblock(p, page, "block name", "text", "options")

This function fills a specific block on a page with text. ■ PDFlib 5 PDI or PPS, PDFlib 6 PDI or PPS

Page	Page handle of an imported PDF from PDF_open_pdi_page().
Block name	The name of the block from the imported PDF that will be used to place text into.
Text	A string of text to be placed into a texblock.
Options	Options can be set to control several aspects of the text.

	Encoding	Set the encoding of the font.
	Embedding	If set to true the font will be embedded into PDF.

This function will only work with PDFlib 5 PDI or PPS and PDFlib 6 PDI or PPS.

PDF_fill_imageblock($p, page, "block name", "image handle", "options")

This function fills a specific block on a page with an image.	PDFlib 5 PDI or PPS, PDFlib 6 PDI or PPS

Page	Page handle of an imported PDF from PDF_open_pdi_page().
Block name	The name of the block from the imported PDF that will be used to place the image into.
Image Handle	An image handle created from PDF_load_image().
Options	Options can be set to control several aspects of the image.

Rotate	The number of degrees to rotate the line.
Orientate	The orientation of the image, north, south, east and west.

This function will only work with PDFlib 5 PDI or PPS and PDFlib 6 PDI or PPS.

PDF_fill_pdfblock($p, $page, "block name", "pdf handle", "options")

This function fills a specific block on a page with a PDF.	PDFlib 5 PDI or PPS, PDFlib 6 PDI or PPS

Page	Page handle of an imported PDF from PDF_open_pdi_page().
Block name	the name of the block from the imported PDF that will be used to place text into.
PDF handle	A PDF handle created from PDF_open_pdi().
Options	Options can be set to control several aspects of the image.

Rotate	The number of degrees to rotate the line.
Orientate	The orientation of the image, north, south, east and west.

This function will only work with PDFlib 5 PDI or PPS and PDFlib 6 PDI or PPS.

PDF_findfont($p, "fontname", "encoding", embed)

This function is used to locate and load a font. `PDFlib 5, PHP4`

Fontname	The name of the font to use.
Encoding	Sets the encoding of the font.
Embed	If this is set to 0 the font will not be embedded. If set to 1 the font will be embedded into the PDF.

This function will work with PDFlib 5 and PDFlib precompiled with PHP4. It has been depreciated in PDFlib 5 and replaced in PDFlib 6 with PDF_load_font().

PDF_fit_image($p, image handle, x, y, "options")

This function will place an image opened by PDF_load_image() at the x, y position. `PDFlib 5, PDFlib 6, PHP4, PHP5`

Image handle	An image handle created by PDF_load_image().		
X	The x position of image on document.		
Y	The y position of image on document.		
Options	Options can be set to control several aspects of the image.		
	adjustpage	If true the current PDF page will adjust around the image.	
	scale	Sets the horizontal and vertical scaling factors with two floating numbers. If both are equal just one number is needed.	
	rotate	The number of degrees to rotate the line.	
	orientate	The orientation of the image, north, south, east and west.	

This function will work with PDFlib 5, PDFlib 6, PDFlib precompiled with PHP4 and PDFlib precompiled with PHP5.

PDF_fit_pdi_page($p, page, x, y, "options")

This page will place an imported PDF onto a page. `PDFlib 5 PDI or PPS, PDFlib 6 PDI or PPS`

Page	The page handle of the PDF opened with `PDF_open_pdi_page()`.
X	The x position of the PDF.
Y	The y position of the PDF.
Options	Options can be set to control several aspects of the placed PDF.

This function will only work with PDFlib 5 PDI or PPS and PDFlib 6 PDI or PPS.

PDF_fit_textflow($p, *textflow handle, llx, lly, urx, ury, "options"*)

This functions places a textflow handle created by `PDF_create_textflow()` into a rectangle.

PDFlib 6, PHP5

Textflow handle	A textflow handle created by `PDF_create_textflow()`.
Llx	The lower left x position.
Lly	The lower left y position.
Urx	The upper right x position
Ury	The upper right y position.

This function will work with PDFlib 6 and PDFlib precompiled with PHP5.

PDF_fit_textline($p, *"text", x, y, "options"*)

This function displays a line of text with the ability to set variable options.

PDFlib 5, PDFlib 6, PHP5

Text	A string of text to be placed onto the PDF.	
X	The starting x position on the page.	
Y	The starting y position on the page.	
Options	Options can be set to control several aspects of the text.	
	`rotate`	The number of degrees to rotate the line.
	`font`	The name of the font to be used.
	`fontsize`	Number representing size of font.

This function will work with PDFlib 5, PDFlib 6 and PDFlib precompiled with PHP5. This function will not work with PDFlib precompiled with PHP4.

PDF_get_buffer(p)

This function gathers the PDF information in a binary format from the functions that were called until the PDF_get_buffer() is used.

PDFlib 5, PDFlib 6, PHP4, PHP5

This function will work with PDFlib 5, PDFlib 6, PDFlib precompiled with PHP4 and PDFlib precompiled with PHP5.

PDF_lineto(p, x, y)

This function will draw a line from a previous point to the x, y position.

PDFlib 5, PDFlib 6, PHP4, PHP5

X	The x position of the point to draw line to.
Y	The y position of the point to draw line to.

This function will work with PDFlib 5, PDFlib 6, PDFlib precompiled with PHP4 and PDFlib precompiled with PHP5.

PDF_load_font(p, *"font name"*, *"encoding"*, *"options"*)

This function is used to locate and load a font.

PDFlib 5, PDFlib 6, PHP5

Fontname	The name of the font to use.	
Encoding	Sets the encoding of the font.	
Options	Options can be set to control several aspects of the font.	
Options	embedding	If set to true the font will be embedding.
	Fontstyle	Options can be set to control the style of the font normal, bold, italic, bolditalic. This will only work with TrueType or OpenType fonts.

This function will work with PDFlib 5, PDFlib 6 and PDFlib precompiled with PHP5. For those using PDFlib precompiled with PHP4 you will have to use PDF_findfont().

PDF_load_image(p, *"image type"*, *image file*, *"options"*)

This function opens up an image file on disk or an image created in memory.

PDFlib 5, PDFlib 6, PHP4, PHP5

Image type	Specify the image type with bmp, ccitt, gif, jpeg, png, raw, or tiff. This can also be set to "auto" to automatically determine file type.
Image file	The file name of the image to be opened.
Options	Options can be set to control several aspects of the image.

This function will work with PDFlib 5, PDFlib 6, PDFlib precompiled with PHP4 and PDFlib precompiled with PHP5.

PDF_makespotcolor($p, "spot color name")

This function locates a spot color in PDFlibs built-in catalog or creates a spot color based on the current fill color.

PDFlib 5, PDFlib 6, PHP5

Spot color name	Name of the spot color in built-in catalog or name of the color that will be created.

This function will work with PDFlib 5, PDFlib 6 and PDFlib precompiled with PHP5. This function will not work with PDFlib precompiled with PHP4.

PDF_moveto($p, x, y)

This function set the position to a certain x, y position.

PDFlib 5, PDFlib 6, PHP4, PHP5

	X	The x position.
	Y	The y position.

This function will work with PDFlib 5, PDFlib 6, PDFlib precompiled with PHP4 and PDFlib precompiled with PHP5.

PDF_new()

This function creates a new PDF.   PDFlib 5, PDFlib 6, PHP4, PHP5

This function will work with PDFlib 5, PDFlib6, PDFlib precompiled with PHP4 and PDFlib precompiled with PHP5.

PDF_open_file($p, "filename")

This function begins a new PDF document.   PDFlib 5, PHP4

Filename	If this option has been set with a filename the document will be created on disk. If the filename is not given the document will be created in memory.

This function will work with PDFlib 5 and PDFlib precompiled with PHP4. It has been replaced in PDFlib 6 with PDF_begin_document().

PDF_open_pdi($p, *filename*, *"options"*, *0*)

This function imports a PDF to be used within a created document.	PDFlib 5 PDI or PPS, PDFlib 6 PDI or PPS

Filename	The name of the file to be imported.	
Options	Options can be set to control several aspects of the opening of the PDF.	
	password	Sets the master password to be used when opening a protected PDF.

This function will only work with PDFlib 5 PDI or PPS and PDFlib 6 PDI or PPS.

PDF_open_pdi_page($p, *"PDF handle"*, *page number*, *"options"*)

This function is used to open a specific page from an imported PDF.	PDFlib 5 PDI or PPS, PDFlib 6 PDI or PPS

PDF handle	The PDF handle of the imported PDF created by PDF_open_pdi().
Page number	The number of the page to be opened.
Options	Options can be set to control several aspects of the PDF.

This function will only work with PDFlib 5 PDI or PPS and PDFlib 6 PDI or PPS.

PDF_setcolor($p, *"fstype"*, *"color type"*, *color1*, *color2*, *color3*, *color4*)

This function sets the current color.	PDFlib 5, PDFlib 6, PHP4, PHP5

Fstype	Specifies to fill, stroke or fillstroke. The value both which is equal to fillstroke is depreciated since PDFlib 5.

Color type	Specifies the color type to be used gray, rgb, cmyk, spot, pattern, iccbasedgray, iccbasedrgb, iccbasedcmyk, or lab.
Color1	Sets the first color value.
Color2	Sets the second color value. In PDFlib 6 if the color value is not used it must be set to 0.
Color3	Sets the third color value. In PDFlib 6 if the color value is not used it must be set to 0.
Color4	Sets the forth color value. In PDFlib 6 if the color value is not used it must be set to 0.

This function will work with PDFlib 5, PDFlib 6, PDFlib precompiled with PHP4 and PDFlib precompiled with PHP5.

PDF_set_info($p, "info field", "value")

This function fills the document information with specific information.

PDFlib 5, PDFlib 6, PHP4, PHP5

Info field	Name of the document information field.

Value	The value to fill the document information field.
Subject	Tubject of the created PDF.
Title	Title of the PDF.
Keywords	A list of keywords.

This function will work with PDFlib 5, PDFlib 6, PDFlib precompiled with PHP4 and PDFlib precompiled with PHP5.

PDF_setfont($p, font handle, font size)

This function set the font from the font handle provided by PDF_findfont() or PDF_load_font().

PDFlib 5, PDFlib 6, PHP4, PHP5

Font handle	The handle created by by PDF_findfont() or PDF_load_font().
Font size	Number representing size of font

This function will work with PDFlib 5, PDFlib 6, PDFlib precompiled with PHP4 and PDFlib precompiled with PHP5.

PDF_set_parameter($p, "parameter", "value")

The function sets one of several parameters of PDFlib.

PDFlib 5, PDFlib 6, PHP4, PHP5

Parameter	Parameter that will be set.
Value	The value that will be set in the parameter.

This function will work with PDFlib 5, PDFlib 6, PDFlib precompiled with PHP4 and PDFlib precompiled with PHP5.

PDF_set_text_pos($p, x, y)

This function sets the text at a given x, y position.

PDFlib 5, PDFlib 6, PHP4, PHP5

X	The x position.
Y	The y position.

This function will work with PDFlib 5, PDFlib 6, PDFlib precompiled with PHP4 and PDFlib precompiled with PHP5.

PDF_show($p, "text")

This function prints a string of text. Position of text must be set prior.

PDFlib 5, PDFlib 6, PHP4, PHP5

Text	A string of text to be printed.

This function will work with PDFlib 5, PDFlib 6, PDFlib precompiled with PHP4 and PDFlib precompiled with PHP5.

PDF_show_xy($p, "text", x, y)

This function prints a string of text at a given position.

PDFlib 5, PDFlib 6, PHP4, PHP5

Text	A string of text to be printed at the given position.
X	The x position of the text string.
Y	The y position of the text string.

This function will work with PDFlib 5, PDFlib 6, PDFlib precompiled with PHP4 and PDFlib precompiled with PHP5.

PDF_setlinewidth($p, width$)

This function sets the line width.

PDFlib 5, PDFlib 6, PHP4, PHP5

Width	Number representing the thickness of the line.

This function will work with PDFlib 5, PDFlib 6, PDFlib precompiled with PHP4 and PDFlib precompiled with PHP5.

PDF_set_value($p, "parameter", value$)

The function sets one of several parameters of PDFlib with a numerical value.

PDFlib 5, PDFlib 6, PHP4, PHP5

Parameter	Parameter that will be set.
Value	The numerical value that will be set in the parameter.

This function will work with PDFlib 5, PDFlib 6, PDFlib precompiled with PHP4 and PDFlib precompiled with PHP5.

Index

Printed in the United Kingdom
by Lightning Source UK Ltd.
112088UKS00001B/400